30 DAYS TO SUCCESS IN REAL ESTATE

FAST TRACK YOUR CAREER IN REAL ESTATE

RITA D. SANTAMARIA

PRESIDENT
CHAMPIONS SCHOOL OF REAL ESTATE, INC.

THOMSON

SOUTH-WESTERN

Australia · Canada · Mexico · Singapore · Spain · United Kingdom · United States

THOMSON

SOUTH-WESTERN

30 Days to Success in Real Estate: A Comprehensive Schedule for the NEW Real Estate Associate
Rita Santamaria

**Vice President/
Editorial Director**
Jack Calhoun

**Vice President/
Editor-in-Chief**
Dave Shaut

Acquisitions Editor
Scott Person

Developmental Editor
Jennifer Warner

Marketing Manager
Mark Linton

Production Editor
Todd McCoy

Production Manager
Patricia Matthews Boies

Manufacturing Coordinator
Charlene Taylor

Printer
West Group
Eagan, Minnesota

Cover Designer
Rik Moore

For permission to use material from this text or product, submit a request online at http://www.thomsonrights.com Any additional questions about permissions can be submitted by email to thomsonrights@thomson.com

For more information, contact South-Western
5191 Natorp Boulevard
Mason, Ohio 45040

Or you can visit our Internet site at: http://www.swlearning.com

How to "Fast Track" Your Career Using
30 Days to Success in Real Estate

Use this journal-style workbook to help fast track your career success in residential or commercial real estate! This guidebook was created specifically to give the brand new or neophyte real estate agent a jumpstart to his or her career.

Starting with financial goals, you, the real estate agent will receive direction as to how many contacts and listings you should obtain to reach your anticipated goal. This book offers financial worksheets and thought-provoking checklists that will guide you toward reaching your financial goals and help you track your progress on a day-to-day basis. By working this proven 30-day plan to success in real estate, you will also establish the essential network you will need to step ahead with confidence.

Each daily plan consists of a definitive list of tasks the agent must accomplish. By completing these daily tasks, from day 1 to day 30, the agent will build a successful career. Learn when to send mailings to your clients, schedule and hold Open Houses, cold call, send "Notice of Listing" cards, organize home inspection tours, and send cards for promotions, among other things. Learn what to say in your calls or correspondence to clients. By using the Daily Summaries, you will realize your accomplishments for each day and plan for the next! Helpful hints for your career in real estate from professional attire to scheduling free time for yourself, will put you on the fast track to success in real estate!

To apply these same tools in your commercial real estate career, simply change the term "homeowner" to "landlord" or "owner" throughout the daily planner. Experienced agents who desire more business can also use this book and go "back to the basics" that are in *30 Days to Success* to get the additional listings deserved.

You have your license, now put yourself in the driver's seat! Congratulations on choosing the "Fast Track" to success in real estate!

The first step in your real estate career should be the preparation of goals. Please take time now to complete the next few pages: I wanted to give you an example to help fill this out. I want you to **SUCCEED!** Rita Santamaria

Financial Goals

Example

If I had $100 extra right now, I would use it for:

Description	**Cost**
a. _____	$ _____
b. _____	$ _____
c. _____	$ _____

If I had an additional $1,000 right now, I would use it for.

d. _____	$ _____
e. _____	$ _____
f. _____	$ _____
g. _____	$ _____

If I had an additional $5,000 right now, I would use it for:

h. _____	$ _____
i. _____	$ _____
j. _____	$ _____
k. _____	$ _____
l. _____	$ _____

$$$

1.	Just to pay my bills each year, I must earn		$ _____
2.	From the items I want on the list above, I must earn		$ _____
3.	So, really, during the next 12 months, I have to earn	(Line 1 + Line 2)	$ _____
4.	That works out to be monthly earnings of	(Line 3/12)	$ _____
5.	Of my monthly earnings, 60% should come from listings sold	(Line 4 x .60)	$ _____
6.	Of my monthly earnings, 40% should come from sales made	(Line 4 x .40)	$ _____

Copyright 2005

What do I have to do to achieve my listing income?

7.   In my market area, the average listing commission is $_____

                            (Get this figure from your broker)

8.   So, I must have the following number of monthly listings sold:_____

9.   If only 75% of my listings sell, I have to get _____ listings.

10.   It may take _____ listing appointments to get a listing.

                Historically given

11.   So I have to go on _____ listing appointments per year to get a listing.

                (Line 9 x Line 10) (/12 mo)

12.   It may take _____ calls to get each listing appointment.

                Given see Goals-3

13.   So I have to make _____ calls each month.

                (Line 11 x Line 12) (/) 12

14.   And I have to make _____ calls each week.

                (Line 13 / Line 4)

15.   And I have to make _____ calls each day.

                (Line 14 / 5 days)

What do I have to do to achieve my sales income?

16.   In my market area, the average sales commission is $_____.

                          (Get this number from your broker)

17.   So, I've got to make _____ sales each month to make my goal.

                (Line 6 / Line 16)

18.   So, I've got to make _____ in sales each week to make my goal.

                (Line 16 / 4)

19.   It takes about _____ property showings to a qualified buyer to make a sale.

                Historically given

20.   So, I must show _____ properties each month.

                (Line 19 x 17)

21.   So, I must show _____ properties each week.

                (Line 19 / 4)

The first step in your real estate career should be the preparation of goals. Please take time now to complete the next few pages: I wanted to give you an example to help fill this out. I want you to **SUCCEED!** Rita Santamaria

Financial Goals

Example

If I had $100 extra right now, I would use it for:

Description	**Cost**
a. _____	$ _____
b. _____	$ _____
c. _____	$ _____

If I had an additional $1,000 right now, I would use it for.

d. _____	$ _____
e. _____	$ _____
f. _____	$ _____
g. _____	$ _____

If I had an additional $5,000 right now, I would use it for:

h. _____	$ 5,000
i. _____	$ _____
j. _____	$ _____
k. _____	$ _____
l. _____	$ _____

$$

1.	Just to pay my bills each year, I must earn		$ 60,000
2.	From the items I want on the list above, I must earn		$ 5,000
3.	So, really, during the next 12 months, I have to earn	(Line 1 + Line 2)	$ 65,000
4.	That works out to be monthly earnings of	(Line 3/12)	$ 5416.67
5.	Of my monthly earnings, 60% should come from listings sold	(Line 4 x .60)	$ 3,250
6.	Of my monthly earnings, 40% should come from sales made	(Line 4 x .40)	$ 21,66.67

What do I have to do to achieve my listing income?

7.   In my market area, the average listing commission is $_____3000_____   **$200,000   Sales price**
            (Get this figure from your broker)   **x   .015**
                                                              3,000

8.   So, I must have the following number of monthly listings sold:_____1_____   **or 13/ year**
            Line 5 x 12 mo. (/) line 7 (/) .75

9.   If only 75% of my listings sell, I have to get _____17 1/3_____ listings/year   **1) 3250 (x) 12**   **2)** $\frac{39000}{3000}$ **= $\frac{13}{75\%}$ = 17**
                                                                     3000

10.   It may take _____3_____ listing appointments to get a listing.   **52 (/) 12 = 4.3/mo.**
            Historically given

11.   So I have to go on _____52_____ listing appointments per year   to get a listing.   **52 (/) 12 = 4.3/mo.**
            (Line 9 x Line 10) (/12 mo)

12.   It may take _____100_____ calls to get each listing appointment.
            Given see Goals-3

13.   So I have to make _____433_____calls each month. $\frac{5200}{12}$ **= 433**
            (Line 11 x Line 12) (/) 12

14.   And I have to make _____108_____ calls each week.   **433**
            (Line 13 / Line 4)   **4 weeks in a month**

15.   And I have to make _____22_____ calls each day. $\frac{108}{5}$ **= 21.6 = 22**
            (Line 14 / 5 days)

This is the most crucial # <u>15</u>!

What do I have to do to achieve my sales income?

16.   In my market area, the average sales commission is $ _____3000_____.
            (Get this number from your broker)

17.   So, I've got to make _____1_____ sales each month to make my goal. $\frac{2166.67}{3000}$ **= .72 = 1**
            (Line 6 / Line 16)

18.   So, I've got to make _____$750_____ in sales each <u>week</u> to make my goal. $\frac{\$3000}{4\ weeks}$
            (Line 16 / 4)

19.   It takes about _____8_____ property showings to a qualified buyer to make a sale.
            Historically given

20.   So, I must show _____8_____ properties each month.
            (Line 19 x 17)

21.   So, I must show _____2_____ properties each week.
            (Line 19 / 4)   **An Easy Goal!**

Contract

(with your face in the mirror)

I, _____ , BEING OF SOUND MIND HAVE DETERMINED MY CAREER GOALS VOLUNTARILY, AND PERSONALLY. I NOW FORMALLY COMMIT TO THE FOLLOWING:

1. During my training period, I will faithfully complete the program set forth in this book.

2. In the next 12 months, I will earn $ _____.

3. I will obtain _____ listings each month.

4. I will go on _____ listing appointments each week.

(Line 11 / 4)

5. I will make _____ listing calls each week.

(Line 14)

6. I will make _____ sales each month.

7. I will show _____ properties each week.

(Line 18 / 4)

If I begin to fall behind, I now request that my broker and/or mentor remind me of this commitment and prod me to stay on schedule so that I can give myself and my family those things which we want and deserve.

_____   _____
Date   Agent's Signature

I acknowledge receipt of this contract. I am committed to your success, and will help you to stay on course.

_____   _____
Date   Broker's Signature

I acknowledge receipt of this contract. I am committed to your success.

_____   _____
Date   Mentor's Signature

*A mentor is a person you respect and who desires to see you succeed.

(Please make 2 photocopies of this contract. Give one copy to your broker and one copy to you "mentor".)

100 Contracts = 1 Listing Appointment
3 Listing Appointments = 1 Listing

Your First Day

MONDAY

8:30-10:00 Many offices reserve Monday morning for sales meeting and caravan of new listings. If your office does not have a sales meeting, use this time to meet with your new associates, enjoy some coffee, and to begin to get "moved in" to your new surroundings.

10:00-12:00 "Caravan" or "Property Tour". The caravan is extremely important since you can't sell unless you know your product. Agents travel to each new residential listing, inspect it carefully, and complete a report on the property as to condition, price and recommendations. If your office does not have a caravan, ask your broker to give you the information on several new listings the office has taken. Take this time to go out to inspect the properties.

12:00-1:00 Lunch

1:00-1:30 Apply for membership at your local associations.

1:30-5:00 Learn how to use office telephone system. Order your business cards. Check with broker or associates about the design requirements and the best place to have them printed.

Included with this book are copies of 2 cards: (See pages A-5, A-8) "Notice of Listing" cards and "Notice of Sale" cards. If your company does not have cards in stock, paste your company logo on the cards, and take them to the local copy company. Order 100 of each and ask them to run them immediately, if possible. You need them for tomorrow afternoon.

Monday Evening

1. If you are married, go through this book with your spouse. Discuss the hours involved. Gain his/her commitment to support your efforts and get a signature on Page 1-4.

2. Prepare a list of 100 friends and acquaintances with addresses and phone number. See next page.

3. Call a friend for lunch tomorrow.

List of Friends, Acquaintances, Centers of Influence, Prospects

Name	Address	Phone	Date Mailed	Date Called

List of Friends, Acquaintances, Centers of Influence, Prospects

Name	Address	Phone	Date Mailed	Date Called

Daily Summary

I have attained my goal for Monday by:	Yes	No
Attending sales meeting;	_____	_____
Inspecting the homes on Property Tour:	_____	_____
Completing application to Local Association; Scheduling MLS orientation	_____	_____
Ordering business cards;	_____	_____
Ordering notice of listing and notice of sale cards;	_____	_____
Preparing list of friends, acquaintances, prospects & COI's;	_____	_____
Making an appointment for lunch with a friend;	_____	_____
Putting uncompleted tasks on next day's agenda	_____	_____
Having a beneficial day.	_____	_____

General comments or questions: _____

_____

_____

_____

For your Spouse or significant other:

STATEMENT OF SUPPORT

I care that _____ be successful in real estate sales. I know that often there will be long hours; and that the first 30 days will be crucial.

I now commit to give moral support and encouragement, to sacrifice my wishes and to help whenever I can, because I am committed to your success!

_____
Signature

Day Two

TUESDAY

8:30-11:30	Organize your office listing book. The listing book is arranged by price. Since you will need to inspect these listings, however, first arrange the sheets by geographical location: North, South, East and West. (You will need to update your book weekly).
11:30-12:00	Write cards to the first 5 friends on your prepared list. (Page 1-2) (For an example of what to say, see Page A-1)
12:00-1:00	Have lunch with a friend. Let your friend know that you are working in Real Estate and that you would welcome any business that he or she might send your way. Then "cool it" and have a friendly lunch.
1:00-3:00	Select a new listing from the bulletin board. For best results, the home should be in a subdivision in the medium price range that has a good volume of turnover. Get the permission of the listing agent, and then send out 20 "Notice of Listing" cards to one of two streets in that neighborhood, using the Criss-Cross Directory. You will be contacting these owners by phone on Day 4. Enter their names, addresses and phone numbers on Page 4-2.
3:00-3:30	Take" Announcement" cards and "Notice of Listing" cards to the post office.
3:30-4:00	Borrow a real estate book from your broker on forms of financing.
4:00-5:00	Purchase the following supplies. Please check them off as you get them: From Hardware Store: (Place these in a small box in your automobile trunk.)

        ____ Hammer
        ____ Screwdriver
        ____ Pliers
        ____ Flashlight and batteries
        ____ Sign Bolts
        ____ Electronic measuring device
        ____ 20 foot steel tape measure
        ____ 50 or 100 foot tape measure
        ____ Polaroid Camera/Digital Camera
        ____ Key map

From the office supply Store:
        ____ Paper clips
        ____ 3' x 5" index cards (min. 200)
        ____ 3" x 5" card box
        ____ Financial calculator
        ____ Small notebook for pocket or purse _Appointment calendar book
        ____ Roll of scotch tape
        ____ Small "Rolodex" or other phone locator

**4:00-5:00
(con't)**
Your broker should have furnished you with a mortgage amortization book or factor card. If not, ask for one and learn how to use it.

You should go to the post office and buy at least 200 stamps for post cards, and at least 100 First Class mail stamps.

Technology Tools:

    a.   Set up e-mail address
    b.   Desktop computer (and/or) Laptop Computer
    c.   Software to create marketing material
    d.   Purchase access to MLS at home from local association of realtors
    e.   Purchaser a day timer or Palm PAD product to keep appointments updated
    f.   Contact management software
    g.   Pay dues and membership to board and MLS
    h.   Obtain lockbox keypad or learn how to use Palm device for that procedure
    i.   Cell phone (and/or) pager
    j.   Printer for computer (preferably laser to ink-jet)
    k.   Purchase high-speed internet access

**Tuesday
Evening:**
Read for at least 1 hour the real estate book you borrowed from your broker today to review loan program requirements.

Call a friend and get a lunch appointment for tomorrow.

Daily Summary

I have attained my goal for Tuesday by: Yes   No

      Organizing my office listing book;   _____   _____

      Sending announcements to 5 friends;   _____   _____

      Having lunch with a friend;   _____   _____

      Sending "Notice of Listing" cards to 20 Owners;   _____   _____

      Purchasing "tools of my trade";   _____   _____

      Reading for one hour;   _____   _____

      Arranging a lunch appointment with a friend for tomorrow;   _____   _____

      Putting unfinished tasks on next day's agenda   _____   _____

      Having a beneficial day.   _____   _____

Comments or questions: _____

_____

_____

_____

Today I Developed the Following Prospects:

Name	Phone	Address	Buyer Seller	Source

$$

I am Totally Committed to My Success!

Day Three

WEDNESDAY

8:30-9:00   Meet with your Broker and order 15 sign "riders" which attach to your company real estate signs. These riders will help you get calls on your own listings, and will keep your name before the public. Allow 3 weeks for delivery. Your broker will tell you how to do this.

Sample Copy:

> **Beth Brown**
> **REALTOR-ASSOCIATE**
> **893-4484**

Get the names of four mortgage lenders from your broker and place those names on Page 3-2. Call one for an appointment at 1:00

9:00-12:00   Visit 10 listings in a geographical area. Always call first for an appointment. List the addresses in the order of travel below.

Record of Listings Inspected

Address	Price	Comments
_____	_____	_____
_____	_____	_____
_____	_____	_____
_____	_____	_____
_____	_____	_____
_____	_____	_____
_____	_____	_____
_____	_____	_____
_____	_____	_____

12:00-1:00   Have lunch with a friend.
My friend's name is: _____

1:00-2:00   Visit one of the mortgage lenders on the list below. Let the loan officer know that you will be working full-time in the business, and that you look forward to a good working relationship.

Name of Firm	Loan Officer	Phone #
_____	_____	_____
_____	_____	_____
_____	_____	_____
_____	_____	_____
_____	_____	_____

2:30-3:00   Write cards to next five friends on the list of Page 1-2.

3:00-5:00   Select a recent sale from the SOLD board. For best results, pick a home in a subdivision with a good amount of activity and in a medium price range. With the permission of the Salesperson involved, send 20 "Notice of Sale" cards to one or two streets in the neighborhood using the Criss-Cross Directory. List the names of the owners in the space provided on Page 5-3. (Criss-Cross is also available in software form)

5:00-6:00   Change into comfortable shoes, leave on business attire*. Have business cards in your jacket pocket and organize your marketing "free gift".

6:00-7:00   Tonight we will visit potential customers for the first time. Walk through your neighborhood and talk with at least 7 owners. Have a small gift to hand out. A pen or a note pad will do fine. If you don't live in an area that makes this easy to do, pick a neighborhood nearby. (For an example of what to say, see Page A-10) List the names and addresses of neighbors you visited on Page 3-3.

Record of Neighborhood Visit

Name	Address	Comments

_____

_____

_____

_____

_____

_____

Send thank you cards to each. Note: For an example of an excellent type of thank you card, see Page A-34.

7:00-8:00   Organize the inspection of listings for tomorrow as shown on Page 4-1. Call for the appointments tonight.

Business Attire for:

      MEN: *A dark suit or sport jacket, white dress shirt, conservative necktie, dress slacks, dark socks (matching pants), and polished shoes. Black or gray are the preferred color of suits. For a more casual look, a blue sports jacket, khaki slacks, white dress shirt, and matching dark socks are appropriate; or, a golf shirt and slacks are fine.*

    WOMEN: *Two piece suits or skirt and matching blouse with blazer, panty hose, clean and polished pumps. (a less feminine look with minimal jewelry is more appropriate). Slacks and blouse are acceptable in today's more business casual society.*

Daily Summary

I have attained my goal for Wednesday by: Yes   No

    Ordering 15 sign riders;   _____   _____

    Visiting 15 listings in one area of my community;   _____   _____

    Having lunch with a friend;   _____   _____

    Talking with a loan officer;   _____   _____

    Sending announcements to 5 friends;   _____   _____

    Sending Notice of Sale cards to 20 homeowners;   _____   _____

    Visiting 7 owners in my neighborhood;   _____   _____

    Organizing home inspection tour for tomorrow;   _____   _____

    Putting unfinished items on next day's agenda   _____   _____

    Having a beneficial day.   _____   _____

Comments or questions: _____

_____

_____

Today I Developed the Following Prospects:

Name	Phone	Address	Buyer Seller	Source

$$$

I am Totally Committed to My Success!

Day Four

THURSDAY

8:30-9:00   Meet with your Broker and discuss your progress. Go over each day's work to date. Go over a sample of a completed listing agreement package.

9:00-12:00   Visit 10 listings in a new geographical area. Always call first for an appointment. List the addresses in the order of travel below:

Address	Price	Comments

12:00-1:00   Lunch

1:00-1:30   Write cards to the next 5 friends on the prepared list on Pages 1-2 and 1-3.

1:30-2:30   Select a recent listing from the "Just Listed" board. For best results, the home should be in a subdivision in the medium price range, and which has a good volume of turnover. Get the permission of the listing agent, and then send out 20 "Notice of Listing cards" to one or two streets in that neighborhood, using the Criss-Cross Directory. You will be contacting these owners by phone on Day 6. Enter their names, addresses and phone numbers on Pages 6-1 and 6-2.

2:30-5:00   Review the complete listing package you received from your broker. Then "list" your personal residence or that of a friend, using all the required forms. You will turn it in to your broker tomorrow morning for review.

5:00-6:00   Stay in the office and take "after hours" property calls.

6:00-7:00   While in the office call 10 of the homeowners listed below to whom you mailed "Notice of Listing" cards on Day 2.

For an example of what you might say on a typical call, see Page A-7.

Record of "Notice of Listing" Cards
*Call these first

Name	Street Address	Phone	Comments
*			
*			
*			
*			
*			
*			
*			
*			
*			

* _____

_____

* _____

_____

* _____

_____

7:00-7:30   Call the five friends to whom you sent announcement cards on Day 2. Get a lunch appointment for tomorrow.

For an example of what to say, see Page A-2.

7:30-8:30   Organize the inspection of listings for tomorrow as shown on Page 5-1. Call for appointments tonight.

Daily Summary

I have attained my goal for Thursday by: Yes   No

    Discussing my progress with my broker;   _____   _____

    Inspecting 15 listings in a different area in my community.   _____   _____

    Sending announcements to 5 friends: _____   _____

    Familiarizing myself with office listing forms;   _____   _____

    "Listing" my own house correctly;   _____   _____

    Calling 10 owners on "Notice of Listing" cards;   _____   _____

    Calling 5 friends, getting a lunch appointment;   _____   _____

    Organizing the inspection of homes for tomorrow;   _____   _____

    Putting unfinished items on next day's agenda   _____   _____

    Having a beneficial day.   _____   _____

Comments or questions: _____

_____

_____

Today I Developed the Following Prospects:

Name	Phone	Address	Buyer Seller	Source

$$$

I am Totally Committed to My Success!

Day Five

FRIDAY

8:30-9:00   Meet with your Broker and discuss your progress.

9:00-12:00   Visit 15 listings in a new geographical area. List the addresses in the order of travel below:

Address	Price	Comments

12:00-1:00   Have lunch with a friend. Let your friend know that you are working in Real Estate and that you would welcome any business that he or she might send your way. Then "Cool it" and have a friendly lunch.

Name of friend: _____

1:00-1:30   Send announcements to the next 5 friends on your prepared list on Pages 1-2 and 1-3.

1:30-2:00   Get daily paper. Make up a list of 10 "For Rent by Owners". (Use Criss-Cross Directory to find names from the phone numbers.

Name	**Phone**	**Comments**

2:00-3:00   Call each "FSBO". Remember to SMILE.
For an example of a typical call, see Page A-5.

3:00-4:00   Visit one of the mortgage lenders shown on Page 3-2. Call for an appointment.

4:00-5:00   If you don't have a good portrait photograph, arrange to have one taken. You will use this photo for ordering a monthly newsletter soon, and will also need it for many uses in the future. Be sure it is of good quality. If you already have a good photo, pick an item from your "to do" list on Page 35. (If you're all caught up, this may be a good time to call on a few homes in your farm area before supper.)

5:00-6:00   Supper

6:00-7:00   Return to home office and call 10 of the homeowners to whom you mailed "Notice of Sale" cards on Day 3.

For an example of what to say, see Page A-9.

Record of "Notice of Sale" Cards
*Call these first

Name	Street Address	Phone	Comments
*			
*			
*			
*			
*			
*			
*			
*			
*			

7:00-7:30   Call 5 friends to whom you sent announcements on Day 3. For an example of what to say, see Page A-2.

Daily Summary

I have attained my goal for Friday by: Yes   No

Discussing my progress with my broker;   _____   _____

Inspecting listings in a new area of the community.   _____   _____

Sending announcements to 5 friends: _____   _____

Having lunch with a friend;   _____   _____

Calling 10 "For Rent by Owners";   _____   _____

Visiting with a mortgage lender;   _____   _____

Having my photograph taken;   _____   _____

Calling 10 owners on "Notice of Sale" Cards;   _____   _____

Putting unfinished items on next day's agenda   _____   _____

Having a beneficial day.   _____   _____

Comments or questions: _____

_____

_____

Today I Developed the Following Prospects:

Name	Phone	Address	Buyer Seller	Source
_____	_____	_____	_____	_____
_____	_____	_____	_____	_____
_____	_____	_____	_____	_____
_____	_____	_____	_____	_____

$$$

I am Totally Committed to My Success!

Day Six

SATURDAY

9:00-10:00   Today we will go door-to door canvassing in the neighborhood where you sent the "Notice of Listing" cards on Day 4. Make up 20 packages to give to owners:

A small gift (Company pen, scratch pad, yardstick, magnet, etc.) A blank company card with your name and phone number typewritten. Your broker will give you a supply of these.

10:00-11:30   Visit the 20 homes in the neighborhood as listed below, and introduce yourself. Statistics show that, for every 100 homes you visit, you should get 5 listing appointments, secure 3 listings, of which 2 will sell.

1. Average listing commission (**) $ _____

2. Total commissions (Line 1 x 2 Sales) $ _____

Hourly rate (Line 2 divided by 8 hours) $ _____/Hour

Dollars per home visited (Line 2 divided by 100) $ _____/Home

Record of "Notice of Listing" Cards & Visits

Name	Street Address	Phone	Comments

_____
_____
_____
_____
_____
_____
_____
_____
_____
_____
_____
_____
_____
_____

11:30-12:30   Send "Thank You" cards to the owners you met. For an example of what to say, see Page A-10.

12:30-1:00   Call the 5 friends to whom you mailed announcements on Day 4.

Daily Summary

I have attained my goal for Saturday by: Yes   No

    Visiting 20 "Notice of Sale" cards;   _____   _____

    Sending "Thank You" cards to friendly owners;   _____   _____

    Calling 5 friends;   _____   _____

    Putting unfinished items on next day's agenda   _____   _____

    Having a beneficial day.   _____   _____

This is the end of your first week in real estate. If you have answered "yes" to the checklist each day, you have had a busy week and may even have developed some prospects. **(If you have answered "no" on more than 50%, you may need to make a stronger commitment to succeed**.) Discuss this with your broker.

We hope you had a beneficial week!

Comments or questions: _____

_____

_____

Today I Developed the Following Prospects:

Name	Phone	Address	Buyer Seller	Source

$$$

I am Totally Committed to My Success!

Day Seven

SUNDAY

Relax today with your family and friends. You deserve it because you have had a busy week!
Please save several sections of the Sunday paper:

Promotions
Wedding Announcements
Births
Classified Ads
Real Estate Section

Write down the person's name, company contact name for further investigation to obtain an address for
the activity on the following page.

Day Eight

MONDAY

8:00-9:00	Get in early and get organized for a new week.
9:00-12:00	This morning review any new sales or listings your office may have gotten in during the last week. Take time to talk to your associates about business that they may have transacted last week, and ask them to tell you a little about what they feel is selling best in your market area.
10:00-11:45	Inspecting listings. You can't sell unless you know your product. This morning, travel to each new residential listing, inspect it carefully, and complete a report on the property as to condition, price and recommendations.
11:45-12:00	Get some purchase contracts & net sheets from your broker. You'll use them tonight.
12:00-1:00	Lunch
1:00-1:30	Send announcements to 5 friends.
1:30-2:30	From Sunday's paper that you saved, make up a list of 10 For Sale By Owners (FSBO's). Use the "Criss-Cross" directory to find the name and address using the phone numbers given.

Record of "For Sale By Owners" Called

Name	Street Address	Phone	Comments

2:00-2:30	Call each FSBO. For an example of what to say, see Page A-13.
3:30-5:00	Send announcements to 5 friends.
1:30-2:30	Ask an associate in the office about one of the buying prospects he or she is working with in a medium price range. Get the following facts:

Approximate ages _____ Married?
# of children _____
Type of work they do _____
Type of house desired: _____ bedrooms _____ baths _____
Price range: $ _____ to? _____
Area of town preferred _____
Willing to commute what distance: _____

Remember always that this type of call is "working statistics", and can be very effective in generating good listings.

Record of Canvassing Calls

Name	**Street Address**	**Phone**	**Comments**
_____	_____	_____	_____
_____	_____	_____	_____
_____	_____	_____	_____
_____	_____	_____	_____
_____	_____	_____	_____
_____	_____	_____	_____
_____	_____	_____	_____
_____	_____	_____	_____
_____	_____	_____	_____
_____	_____	_____	_____

5:00-6:00	Supper

6:00-8:00   Select a listing in the $90,000 price range from your office listing book. Tonight you will write a purchase contract.

Information for Contract #1

Buyer's names:	Eileen & Ben Dover
Purchase Price:	$90,000
Financing:	New FHA mortgage
Personal Property:	range, refrigerator, drapes
Earnest Money:	$1000
Closing date:	45 days from today
Closing costs:	paid as is usual in your area
Discount points:	today's rate

Information for Contract #2

Same as above, except price is $120,000 and financing to be a conventional 80% loan.

Information for Contract #3

Same as above, except that buyer will assume an existing loan of $50,000 and pay cash difference. Transfer fee is $500.

Please prepare for each:

Buyer's statement of costs
Seller's statement of costs
Purchase contract

Do this tonight, even if you're not sure how. This is a learning experience.

You should make yourself completely familiar with the purchase contract, and understand each word and be able to explain it clearly.

Make a list of things you want your Broker to explain. You will be going over these items tomorrow at 9:30.

Daily Summary

I have attained my goal for Monday by:	Yes	No
Attending Sales Meeting;	_____	_____
Inspecting homes;	_____	_____
Sending announcement to 5 friends;	_____	_____
Calling 10 "For Sale By Owners";	_____	_____
Telephone canvassing 10 homeowners;	_____	_____
Writing 3 purchase contracts;	_____	_____
Putting unfinished item on next day's agenda	_____	_____
Having a beneficial day.	_____	_____

Comments or questions: _____

_____

_____

Today I Developed the Following Prospects:

Name	Phone	Address	Buyer Seller	Source
_____	_____	_____	_____	_____
_____	_____	_____	_____	_____
_____	_____	_____	_____	_____
_____	_____	_____	_____	_____

$$

I am Totally Committed to My Success!

Day Nine

TUESDAY

8:30-9:30 Review the work that you did last night on the purchase contract. You should plan to present the work to your broker at 9:30. Make notes about any items you feel you need help on from your broker.

9:30-10:30 Meet with your broker to discuss your progress to date, and to review the contracts you prepared last night.

10:30-11:30 Send card and a copy of the clipping from Sunday's paper to:

> Newlyweds
> Promotions
> Births

Save names and addresses on Page 11-2. You will be calling them on Thursday. For an example of what to say see Page A-3.

11:30-12:00 Send announcements to the next 5 friends on your prepared list on Page 1-3.

12:00-1:00 Lunch. Go to a new place and always give the waiter/waitress your business card.

1:00-2:00 Select a recent sale from the bulletin board. For best results, pick a home in a subdivision with a good level of sale activity in a medium price range. With the permission of the salesperson involved, send 20 "Notice of Sale" cards to one or two streets in the neighborhood using the Criss-Cross Directory. **Be certain to say "Our Company" participated in the sale of..."** List the names of the owners in the space provided on Page 11-3. Take these to the Post office to ensure early delivery.

2:00-2:30 Call 5 of the friends to whom you sent announcement last Friday.

2:30-4:00 Make 10 canvassing calls as described on Page 8-2 at 3:30. For an example of what to say, see Page A-11.

Record of Canvassing Calls

Name	Street Address	Phone	Comments

_____

_____

_____

4:00-5:00   Decide on a civic club to join. * This is a way for you to give back to the community some of what you take from it. It also, very importantly, makes it easy for you to meet new friends.

        The more people you meet, the more successful you will become.

        My Club choice is _____

5:00-6:00   Supper

6:00-7:00   Organize the inspection of office listings for tomorrow as shown on Page 10-1. Call for appointments tonight.

7:00-8:00   Read completely through the text of the listing presentation from Page A-17 through Page A-24. You should re-read and learn pages A-17 to A-20 and be ready to discuss them with your broker tomorrow.

*Possible club choices:

   Rotary, Homeowner's Associations, PTO, Golf or Tennis Association, Political group, Citivans, Toastmasters, Service League, Chamber of Commerce, etc,

Daily Summary

I have attained my goal for Tuesday by: Yes   No

    Reviewing my work on the contracts;   _____   _____

    Meeting with my broker to review contracts;   _____   _____

    Sending cards for promotions, weddings, births;   _____   _____

    Sending announcements to 5 friends;   _____   _____

    Giving my card to the waiter at lunch: _____   _____

    Sending 20 "Notice of Sale" cards;   _____   _____

    Calling friends to whom I have mailed announcements;   _____   _____

    Making 10 calls on a Real Estate Survey;   _____   _____

    Choosing a club to join.   _____   _____

    Organizing the home inspection tour for tomorrow;   _____   _____

    Learning part of the Listing Presentation.   _____   _____

    Putting unfinished items on next day's agenda   _____   _____

    Having a beneficial day.   _____   _____

Comments or questions: _____

_____

_____

Today I Developed the Following Prospects:

Name	Phone	Address	Buyer Seller	Source

$$

I am Totally Committed to My Success!

Day Ten

WEDNESDAY

8:30-9:30   Meet with Broker to discuss your progress. Discuss the selection of a "Farm" area, and get some feedback as to what you should look for in making the selection.

Give a presentation of the first part of your listing presentation narrative.

9:30-10:30   Order a personalized self-adhesive labels from a stationery store:

Compliments of
(your name)
REALTOR-ASSOCIATE
(your company name)

10:30-12:00   Visit 15 listings in a new geographical area of the city. Always call first for an appointment. List the addresses in the order of travel below:

Address	Price	Comments

12:00-1:00   Lunch

1:00-1:30   Get daily paper. Make up a list of 10 "For Rent by Owners". (Use Criss-Cross directory to find names from phone numbers.)

Name	Phone	Comments

1:30-2:30   Call each "FRBO". Remember to SMILE.
For an example of what to say see Page A-5.

2:30-3:30   Select a "Farm" area. You will be THE real estate specialist in the neighborhood.

The selection of a good farm area is important, and should be considered carefully. The ideal area will have at least 200 homes, with prices in the upper-middle ranges. There should be reasonable sales activity in the area. Your broker's help and approval should be secured.

In many areas, you can expect homes to be put up for sale once every 5 years on average. One of 5 homes will be put on the market this year. That's 20%. In a neighborhood of 200 homes, there is a potential of 40 listings. SELECT CAREFULLY.

My farm area will be _____

3:30-5:00   Mail out 20 farm letters to owners in your area. List them on Page 13-1. For an example of what to say see Page A-26.

5:00-6:00   Supper with your family.

6:00-7:00   Get an MLS computer printout. Select 10 listings that expired at least one month ago. Check in the current book or computer to ensure that they have not been relisted. List the names and addresses here:

Record of Expired Listings

Name	Street Address	Phone	Comments

Call each person on the list.
For an example of what to say, see Page A-29.

7:00-7:30   Call the five friends that you mailed to Day 8.

For an example of what to say, see page A-2.

7:30-8:00   Commit to memory Pages A-17 to A-20 of the Listing Presentation.

Daily Summary

I have attained my goal for Wednesday by:

	Yes	No
Discussing my progress with my broker;	_____	_____
Ordering adhesive labels;	_____	_____
Inspecting 15 listings;	_____	_____
Calling 10 "For Rent By Owners";	_____	_____
Selecting a "Farm" area:	_____	_____
Mailing to 20 owners in my "Farm" area;	_____	_____
Calling 10 previously expired listings;	_____	_____
Calling 5 friends from my prepared list;	_____	_____
Learning more of the Listing Presentation;	_____	_____
Putting unfinished tasks on next day's agenda	_____	_____
Having a beneficial day.	_____	_____

Comments or questions: _____

_____

_____

Today I Developed the Following Prospects:

Name	Phone	Address	Buyer Seller	Source
_____	_____	_____	_____	_____
_____	_____	_____	_____	_____
_____	_____	_____	_____	_____

$$

I am Totally Committed to My Success!

Day Eleven

THURSDAY

8:00-9:00   Meet to discuss your progress with your broker. Go over next section of the Listing Presentation.

9:00-10:00   Take a driving tour of your" farm" area. Make notes of addresses of homes now for sale and homes having "sold" signs.

10:00-12:00   Return to the office. Make a complete "Competitive Market Report" on the real estate activity in the area for at least the first year, and arrange it by street. (See Market Report form on Page A-33) If a plat of the neighborhood is available, make a copy and color in the properties that are for sale or have been sold.

12:00-1:00   Lunch

2:00-3:00   Select a new sale from the bulletin board. For best results, the home should be in a subdivision with a good amount of activity and in the medium price range. With the permission of the salesperson involved, send out 20 "Notice of Sale" cards to one of two streets in the neighborhood, using the Criss-Cross Directory. List the names of the owners in the space provided on Page 13-2. Take these to the Post Office to ensure early delivery.

3:00-4:00   From each day's report where you have written in the names of prospects you have generated, transfer the names to copies of the prospect cards as shown on Page A-31, or as provided by your broker.

4:00-5:00   "Free time". Use this time productively to catch up on work you have fallen behind on, to make calls on prospects you've generated, or to take care of other items that will help you to become the success you know you can be.

5:00-6:00   Supper

6:00-7:00   Call "Congratulations" to newlyweds, promotions and births that you mailed to on Day 9. For an example of what to say, see Page A-2.

Record of Congratulation Calls

Name	Event	Phone	Comments

_____

_____

_____

_____

_____

_____

_____

_____

7:00-8:00   Return to the office and call to homeowners listed below to whom you mailed "Notice of Sale" cards on Day 9.

For an example of what to say, see Page A-9.

Record of "Notice of Sale" Cards
*Call these first

Name	Street Address	Phone	Comments
*			
*			
*			
*			
*			
*			

Daily Summary

I have attained my goal for Thursday by:	Yes	No
Discussing my progress with my broker;	_____	_____
Driving through my farm area;	_____	_____
Preparing a Market Report on my farm area;	_____	_____
Sending out 20 "Notice of Sale" Cards;	_____	_____
Visiting a mortgage loan officer:	_____	_____
Calling on Newlyweds, Births, and Promotions;	_____	_____
Calling on 10 Notice of Sale cards;	_____	_____
Putting unfinished tasks on next day's agenda	_____	_____
Having a good day.	_____	_____

Comments or questions: _____

_____

_____

_____

Today I Developed the Following Prospects:

Name	Phone	Address	Buyer Seller	Source

$$\$$$

I am Totally Committed to My Success!

Day Twelve

FRIDAY

8:30-10:00   Meet with your broker to discuss progress to date. Present the contract of Harry Owens that you did on Day 8, as if your broker is the buyer. Please explain buyer's statement, and then go through the Purchase Contract, explaining each section in detail.

Next, present the contract as if your broker is the seller. First explain seller's statement, and then go through the Purchase Contract.

10:00-12:00   Organize a farm book. An 8.5" x 11" loose-leaf notebook is convenient. Make 100 copies of the Homeowner Information sheets as shown on Page A-28.

Divide into streets with tabs. Enter names of the 20 homeowners to whom you sent farm letters on Day 10, which are listed on Page 13-1. You will be visiting these homes tomorrow.

12:00-1:00   Lunch.

1:00-3:00   Visit the Chamber of Commerce. Ask for their files on requests for information from out of towners. Copy down names and addresses of 5 individuals and return to the office. Mail relocation packages which will include the following:

City map
Small gift-pen, pad, etc
Your business card
A short note of welcome

After you have completed this, send out a referral form to a Realtor in their hometown that suggests that the party be contacted about listing their property. Ask your broker how to do this.

Record of Listing Referrals Sent

Name	Address	City, Street, Zip	Pkg. Sent	Ref. Sent

Daily Summary

I have attained my goal for Friday by:	Yes	No
Meeting with my broker to discuss progress;	_____	_____
Presenting Purchase Contract for Harry Owens;	_____	_____
Organizing your "farm" book;	_____	_____
Sending out packages to prospective new residents;	_____	_____
Sending out referrals for listings;	_____	_____
Putting unfinished tasks on next day's agenda	_____	_____
Having a good day.	_____	_____

Comments or questions: _____

_____

_____

_____

Today I Developed the Following Prospects:

Name	Phone	Address	Buyer Seller	Source
___	___	___	___	___
___	___	___	___	___
___	___	___	___	___

$$

I am Totally Committed to My Success!

Day Thirteen

SATURDAY

9:00-10:00   Prepare handouts for homeowners in your farm area to whom you mailed letters on Wednesday. These handouts can be simple items like a company pen, note pads, or a package of flower seed. Attach your business card to the handouts. You should pack at least 20 gifts.

10:00-12:00   Visit the first 20 homeowners in your farm area.

For an example of what to say see Page A-27.

Record of Farm Visits Made

Address	Price	Phone	Comments

12:00-1:00   Return to the office and call 10 of the homeowners listed below to whom you mailed "Notice of Sale" cards on Day 11.

For an example of what to say, see Page A-9.

Record of "Notice of Sale" Cards Mailed
*Call these first

Name	Street Address	Phone	Comments
*			
*			
*			
*			
*			
*			
*			
*			
*			
*			

Daily Summary

I have attained my goal for Saturday by:	**Yes**	**No**
Visiting 20 homeowners in my farm area;	_____	_____
Calling 10 owners on "Notice of Sale" cards;	_____	_____
Putting unfinished tasks on next day's agenda	_____	_____
Having a good day.	_____	_____

Comments or questions: _____

_____

_____

_____

Today I Developed the Following Prospects:

Name	Phone	Address	Buyer Seller	Source

You are now at the end of your second week in real estate. If you have answered "yes" to the checklist each day, you have been busy. You should begin seeing the results of this work before the month has ended.

WE HOPE YOU HAD A GOOD WEEK.

$$$

I am Totally Committed to My Success!

Day Fourteen

SUNDAY

This is a day for your church, your family, and your friends. We hope you enjoy it. From Sunday's paper, please clip and save:

Promotions

Wedding announcements

Births

Classified ads

Day Fifteen

MONDAY

8:30-9:00	Get in the office early to get organized for the new week.
9:00-10:00	Attend sales meeting or review transactions for last week.
10:00-12:00	Inspect new listings to keep you informed when you talk to prospects.
12:00-1:00	Lunch
1:00-1:30	Send announcements to the next 5 friends on your prepared list on Pages 1-2 and 1-3.
1:30-2:30	Using the classified ads from Sunday's paper, clip out 10 "For Sale By Owner" ads. Read a book or listen to a tape on FSBO's

Record of "For Sale By Owners" Called

Address	Price	Comments

2:00-2:30	Call each FSBO. For an example of what to say, see Page A-13.

3:30-5:00   Visit FSBO homes if you have permission.

When you arrive, there are several questions to ask while you are inspecting the property. These questions will help you to gain information, and to establish rapport with the seller. For an example of what to say, see Page A-14.

5:00-6:00   Supper

6:00-8:00   Study and learn the balance of the Listing Presentation. It will be your best tool to a large listing inventory when working with "For Sale By Owners."

Daily Summary

I have attained my goal for Monday by: Yes   No

    Attending sales meeting;   _____   _____

    Inspecting homes;   _____   _____

    Sending announcements to 5 friends: _____   _____

    Calling 10 "For Sale By Owners";   _____   _____

    Visiting "For Sale By Owners" in their homes;   _____   _____

    Learning the balance of my Listing Presentation;   _____   _____

    Putting unfinished tasks on next day's agenda   _____   _____

    Having a good day.

Comments or questions: _____

_____

_____

Today I Developed the Following Prospects:

Name	Phone	Address	Buyer Seller	Source
_____	_____	_____	_____	_____
_____	_____	_____	_____	_____
_____	_____	_____	_____	_____

$$

I am Totally Committed to My Success!

Day Sixteen

TUESDAY

8:30-9:30   In some locations, there is a Board of REALTOR meeting on Tuesdays. If there is one in your area, arrange to attend. If those meetings are held on other days of the week, rearrange your schedule if possible to attend. If there is no meeting today, use this hour as "catch-up time".

9:30-10:30   Arrange to begin receiving 100 issues of a monthly real estate brochure that you send to your "Sphere of influence". It will have your name and photo on the masthead, as well as that of the company. The cost is minimal and will result in substantially increased business for you. A sample newsletter is included at Page A-35.

10:30-12:00   Begin setting up a card file for working with FSBO's in a more organized way. Clip out the ads from Sunday's paper; paste each ad on a separate 3" x 5" file card. See Page A-16.

                     Look up the owner from the phone number section of the Criss-Cross Directory, and fill in the name and address of the owner. Then phone number should be prominently placed in the upper right corner of the card. Your cards will be filed by telephone exchange for quick reference each day when you review the paper for new offerings. Your broker will assist if you need help.

12:00-1:00   Lunch. Give the waitress/waiter you business card and ask for business.

1:00-2:30   Select the price range that you think containing the most buyers. Select an area that contains a reasonable number of homes for sale in that price range. Go out and preview 5 homes (whether listed by your company or others), choosing the one you consider most saleable and write down the reasons why. List the homes you visit below.

Record of Homes Previewed

Address   **Price**   **Comments**

_____

_____

_____

_____

Most Saleable is _____

_____

Why? _____

_____

2:30-4:00   Get the most recent expired listings from MLS. On the next page, enter a list of 10 owners with addresses and phone numbers.

4:00-5:00   Select a new sale from the bulletin board. For best results, pick a home in a subdivision with a good amount of activity and in a medium price range. With the permission of the Salesperson involved, send 20 "Notice of Sale" cards to one or two street in the neighborhood using the Criss-Cross Directory. List the names of the owners in the space provided on Page 19-2. Take these to the Post Office to ensure early delivery.

5:00-6:00   Supper

6:00-7:00   Call 10 expired listings. Be courteous. If they indicate they will relist, with their present broker, be supportive. If they are not relisting, **Get An Appointment.**

For an example of that to say, see Page A-29.

Record of Expired Listing Calls

Name	Street Address	Phone	Comments

7:00-8:00   Call the five friends you mailed cards to yesterday. Get an appointment to take a friend to lunch Thursday.

Daily Summary

I have attained my goal for Tuesday by: Yes   No

Attending the REALTORS meeting, or catching up;   _____   _____

Arranging to receive monthly newsletters for my farm;   _____   _____

Setting up card files for FSBO's: _____   _____

Previewed homes in popular price range;   _____   _____

Sending "Notice of Sale" cards to 20 owners;   _____   _____

Calling 10 expired listings;   _____   _____

Putting unfinished items on next day's agenda   _____   _____

Having a good day.   _____   _____

Comments or questions: _____

_____

_____

Today I Developed the Following Prospects:

Name	Phone	Address	Buyer Seller	Source

$$$

I am Totally Committed to My Success!

Day Seventeen

WEDNESDAY

9:00-10:00   Prepare letters to 20 owners in your farm area. For a sample letter, see Page A-26.

10:00-12:00   Prepare letters to 10 FSBO's from the card files you set up yesterday. List them on Page 20-2. For a sample letter, see Page A-15.

Mail farm letters and FSBO letters now.

12:00-1:00   Lunch. Give the waitress your business card and ask her to send you some business.

1:00-3:30   Set up a "stenographers" notebook with pages for each of the major price ranges of homes. For instance, from $90,000 to $100,000 etc. This will be your book of homes that you have inspected and from which you will be able to discuss the most saleable in each price range. Starting at the front of this book, enter all the homes you've seen into the appropriate section.

Choose another neighborhood that has a number of homes in the popular price range you selected yesterday and preview five homes. Please list those homes below. When you return to the office, determine the most saleable. Put these homes in you notebook.

Record of Homes Previewed

Address	Price	Comments
_____	_____	_____
_____	_____	_____
_____	_____	_____
_____	_____	_____

Most Saleable is _____

_____

Why? _____

_____

3:00-5:00   Get the most recently expired listings from MLS. Enter the names, addresses and phone numbers of the 10 best on the bottom of this page. You will be calling them this evening at 6:00.

5:00-6:00   Supper with your family

6:00-7:00   Call 10 expired listings from the list below. Be courteous. If they indicate they will re-list with their present agent, be supportive. If they don't intend to relist, Get an Appointment. For an example of what to say, see Page A-29.

Record of Expired Listing Calls

Name	Street Address	Phone	Comments

7:00-8:00   Study your listing presentation. Try giving parts of it to your spouse and get feedback on your technique.

Daily Summary

I have attained my goal for Wednesday by:　　　　　　　　**Yes**　　　**No**

Preparing letters to 20 owners in my farm area;　　　　　　_____　_____

Preparing letters to FSBO's;　　　　　　　　　　　　　　_____　_____

Previewing homes in popular price range:　　　　　　　　_____　_____

Calling 10 expired listings;　　　　　　　　　　　　　　_____　_____

Studying my listing presentation;　　　　　　　　　　　_____　_____

Putting unfinished items on next day's agenda;　　　　　　_____　_____

Having a good day.　　　　　　　　　　　　　　　　　_____　_____

Comments or questions: _____

_____

_____

Today I Developed the Following Prospects:

Name	Phone	Address	Buyer Seller	Source

$$

I am Totally Committed to My Success!

Copyright 2005

Day Eighteen

THURSDAY

8:30-9:30	Discuss progress with broker.
	How do you feel about your calls on FSBO's?
	How do you feel about your calls on expireds?
	What are your feelings about the real estate business?

9:30-11:30   Prepare letters to 10 FSBO's from the card files you set up on Day 16. List them on Page 21-2. For an example of what to say, see Page A-15.

11:30-12:00   Mail your FSBO letters to ensure early delivery. Then take your car to the car wash. A clean car makes you feel good, and when you feel good AND look good, you earn money.

12:00-1:00   Have lunch with the friend you talked with on Day 16. Ask for a referral.

1:00-3:00   Select 5 homes to preview in a popular price range. List them below, and also in your steno book of properties you have previewed. Mark those you believe to be most saleable.

Record of Properties Previewed

Address	Price	Comments

Most Saleable is _____

_____

Why? _____

_____

3:00-4:00   Get the most recently expired listings from MLS. Write out a list of 10 owners with addresses and phone numbers on Page 18-2.

4:00-5:00   Read the "Exclusive Right of Sale" agreement for understanding. Write out a "paraphrasing" in lay (non-legal) words. Learn to present it.

5:00-6:00   Supper.

6:00-7:00   Call 10 expired listings shown below. Be courteous. If they indicate they will re-list with their present agent, be supportive. If they are not relisting, **Get an Appointment.** For an example of what to say, see Page A-29.

Record of Expired Listing Calls

Name	Street Address	Phone	Comments

Daily Summary

I have attained my goal for Thursday by: Yes   No

Discussing my progress with my broker;   _____   _____

Preparing and mailing letters to FSBO's;   _____   _____

Getting my car washed;   _____   _____

Previewing 5 homes in a popular price range: _____   _____

Paraphrasing the listing agreement;   _____   _____

Calling 10 expired listings;   _____   _____

Putting unfinished items on next day's agenda;   _____   _____

Having a good day.   _____   _____

Comments or questions: _____

_____

_____

_____

Today I Developed the Following Prospects:

Name	Phone	Address	Buyer Seller	Source

$$$

I am Totally Committed to My Success!

Day Nineteen

FRIDAY

8:30-9:30   Discuss your progress with your broker.
                 Is the work too hard?
                 Is your spouse supportive?
                 Are you ready to continue at this pace?

9:30-12:00   Catch-up time.

                 My catch-up task: _____

12:00-1:00   Lunch.

1:00-3:30   Purchase the Daily Paper. Call 10 "For Rent by Owners". For an example of what to say, see Page A-5.

Record of "For Rent by Owners" Called

Name	Address	Price	Comments

3:00-5:00   Call on 10 "Notice of Sale" cards you mailed Tuesday. For an example of what to say, see Page A-9.

Record of "Notice of Sale" Cards Mailed
*Call these first

Name	Street Address	Phone	Comments
*			
*			
*			
*			
*			
*			
*			
*			
*			
*			
*			

Daily Summary

I have attained my goal for Friday by:	Yes	No
Discussing my progress with my broker;	_____	_____
Catching up on tasks not completed;	_____	_____
Calling 10 "For Rent By Owner's":	_____	_____
Calling 10 "Notice of Sale" cards;	_____	_____
Putting unfinished items on next day's agenda;	_____	_____
Having a good day.	_____	_____

Comments or questions: _____

_____

_____

_____

Today I Developed the Following Prospects:

Name	Phone	Address	Buyer Seller	Source
_____	_____	_____	_____	_____
_____	_____	_____	_____	_____
_____	_____	_____	_____	_____

$$$

I am Totally Committed to My Success!

Day Twenty

SATURDAY

9:00-10:00   Get ready to visit your "farm". Prepare handout for 20 homeowners in your farm area to whom you mailed letters on Wednesday. Attach your business card to a simple gift like a company pen, notepads or a tape measure.

10:00-12:00   Visit 20 homeowners in your farm area. For an example of what to say, see Page A-27. Try to complete a Homeowners Information Sheet for each property, but if owner is reluctant, don't push.

Record of Farm Area Visits Made

Name	Address	Phone	Comments

_____

_____

_____

_____

_____

_____

12:00-1:00   Return to the office and call the FSBO's listed below to whom you mailed letters Wednesday. For an example of what to say, see Page A-13.

Record of "For Sale by Owner" Letters

Name	Address	Phone	Comments

Daily Summary

I have attained my goal for Saturday by: Yes   No

    Visiting 20 homeowners in my farm area;   _____   _____

    Calling on 10 "For Sale by Owner" letters;   _____   _____

    Putting unfinished items on next day's agenda;   _____   _____
    -
    Having a good day.   _____   _____

Comments or questions: _____

_____

_____

_____

Today I Developed the Following Prospects:

Name	Phone	Address	Buyer Seller	Source
_____	_____	_____	_____	_____
_____	_____	_____	_____	_____

You are now ending your 3rd week in Real Estate. You should be starting to see some good things happening by now.

We hope you had a good week!

$$\$$$

I am Totally Committed to My Success!

Day Twenty-One

SUNDAY

Afternoon, sometime between 2:00 and 5:00. Call the FSBO's you mailed on Thursday.

Sunday is an excellent day to talk to owners, particularly if they have had no activity over the weekend. For an example of what to say, see Page A-13.

Record of "For Sale by Owner" Calls Made

Name	Address	Phone	Comments

Day Twenty-Two

MONDAY

8:30-9:00	Get to work early and get organized for the new week.
9:00-10:00	Attend sales meeting or review transactions for last week.
10:00-12:00	Inspect new listings to keep you informed of what's on the market.
12:00-1:00	Lunch
1:00-3:00	Purchase a daily newspaper. List 10 "For Rent by Owners" in the space below using the "Criss-Cross" Directory. Call these FRBO's to get a listing. For an example of a typical call, see Page A-5.

Record of "For Rent by Owners" Called

Name	Address	Phone	Comments

3:00-4:00	From Sunday's paper, clip marriages, promotions, and births. Send cards of congratulations. For an example of what to say, see Page A-3. List the names of 10 of these people on Page 24-2.

4:00-5:00   Look in the "Criss-Cross" Directory for a middle-income apartment complex and enter 10 names at the bottom of this page. Make 10 completed calls to renters. For an example of what to say, see Page A-12. Put the good prospects in your prospect file.

Record of Apartment Renters

Name	Address	Phone	Comments

5:00-6:00   Supper with your family.

6:00-7:00   Catch-up time.

Daily Summary

I have attained my goal for Monday by: Yes   No

Attending sales meeting;   _____   _____

Inspecting new listings on caravan;   _____   _____

Calling 10 For Rent by Owners;   _____   _____

Sending cards on promotions, marriages, births;   _____   _____

Calling 10 renters;   _____   _____

Catching up on unfinished tasks;   _____   _____

Putting unfinished tasks on next day's agenda;   _____   _____

Having a good day.   _____   _____

Comments or questions: _____

_____

_____

_____

Today I Developed the Following Prospects:

Name	Phone	Address	Buyer Seller	Source

$$$

I am Totally Committed to My Success!

Day Twenty-Three

TUESDAY

8:30-9:30   In some locations, there is a Board of REALTOR meeting on Tuesdays. If there is one in your area, arrange to attend. If there is no meeting today, use this hour as "catch-up time".

9:30-11:00   Discuss progress with broker. Do the best you can do on your listing presentation. Try not to use the text sheets except as a reminder.

11:00-12:00   Select a new listing from the bulletin board. For best results, the home should be in a subdivision in the medium price range, which has a good volume of turnover. Get the permission of the listing agent, and then send out 20 "Notice of Listing" cards to one or two streets in that neighborhood, using the Criss-Cross Directory. You will be contacting these owners by phone on Thursday. Enter the name, address, and phone number on Page 25-2.

12:00-1:00   Lunch

1:00-3:00   From Sunday's paper that you saved, make up a list of 10 "For Sale by Owners". Use the Criss-Cross Directory to find the name and address of the owner using the phone number. Call each FSBO. For an example of what to say, see Page A-13.

Record of "For Rent by Owners" Called

Name	Address	Phone	Comments

3:00-5:00   Use this time to visit any FSBO's you make appointments with, or you can use if to catch up on uncompleted tasks from Page 35.

5:00-6:00   Supper with your family.

6:00-7:00   Read the Open House section from "How to List and Sell Real Estate" by Danielle Kennedy, copyright 1984 by Prentice Hall. You'll need the information soon.

Daily Summary

	Yes	No
I have attained my goal for Tuesday by:		
Giving my listing presentation to my broker;	_____	_____
Sending 20 "Notice of Listing" cards to owners;	_____	_____
Calling 10 For Sale by Owners;	_____	_____
Using time to visit FSBO's or to catch up;	_____	_____
Reading about open houses in "How to List and Sell Real Estate";	_____	_____
Putting unfinished tasks on next day's agenda;	_____	_____
Having a good day.	_____	_____

Comments or questions: _____

_____

_____

_____

Today I Developed the Following Prospects:

Name	Phone	Address	Buyer Seller	Source
_____	_____	_____	_____	_____
_____	_____	_____	_____	_____
_____	_____	_____	_____	_____

$$$

I am Totally Committed to My Success!

Day Twenty-Four

WEDNESDAY

8:30-9:00   Discuss progress with broker.

9:00-10:00   Select an active listing in a popular price range on a high traffic street. Discuss with the listing salesman your holding an open house this coming Sunday from 2 to 5 p.m. If the listing salesman agrees, arrange for him/her to call the owners for their approval. Be sure the owners understand that they should leave the house during those hours.

10:00-11:00   Visit the property, and then write an ad for the open house. Have it approved by the listing salesman and by your broker.

11:00-12:00   Select a new listing from the bulletin board. For best results, the home should be in a subdivision in the medium price range, and which has a good volume of turnover. Get the permission of the listing agent, and then send out 20 Notice of Listing cards to one or two streets in that neighborhood, using the Criss-Cross Directory. You will be contacting these owners by phone on Saturday. Enter their names, addresses and phone numbers on Page 27-2.

12:00-1:00   Lunch

1:00-2:00   Call 10 "For Sale by Owners". Try to set at least 3 appointments to visit them in their homes. For an example of what to say, see Page A-13.

Record of "For Sale by Owners" Called

Name	Address	Phone	Comments

2:00-4:00	Use this time to visit FSBO's or for catch-up time for uncompleted items.
4:00-5:00	Mail to next 20 owners in your farm area the letter as shown on Page A-26. List the names on Page 27-1.
5:00-6:00	Supper
6:00-7:00	Call recipients of cards you sent for promotions, marriages and births. For an example of what to say, see Page A-3.

Record of "Congratulations" Calls

Name	Address	Phone	Comments

7:00-8:00	Read about floor duty in "How to List and Sell Real Estate" by Danielle Kennedy copyright 1984 by Prentice Hall.

Daily Summary

I have attained my goal for Wednesday by:	Yes	No
Discuss my progress with my broker;	_____	_____
Select a property for open house;	_____	_____
Write an ad for open house;	_____	_____
Send out 20 "Notice of Listing" cards;	_____	_____
Call 10 FSBO's;	_____	_____
Mail to 20 owners in farm area;	_____	_____
Can on congratulations;	_____	_____
Read about floor duty;	_____	_____
Putting unfinished tasks on next day's agenda;	_____	_____
Having a good day.	_____	_____

Comments or questions: _____

_____

_____

_____

Today I Developed the Following Prospects:

Name	Phone	Address	Buyer Seller	Source

$$$

I am Totally Committed to My Success!

Day Twenty-Five

THURSDAY

8:30-9:00   Prepare for Floor Duty. Floor duty is the privilege of receiving all incoming ad calls during the time of your "duty". You must always prepare to take these calls, and strive to "meet in person every qualified buyer."

You should:
1. Identify all homes in the most recent newspaper ads. Ensure that you have the list of homes in the ads, and that you have the listing information on each.
2. For each home above, select 3 comparable homes to discuss with callers.
3. Have some prospect cards ready.
4. Have "20 Questions to ask ad callers" ready and use them. See Page A-30.

You must ask questions to control the conversation.

9:00-1:00   Floor Duty

The most important thing to remember when taking ad calls is that the telephone should be used only to get the appointment, NOT to sell the property. When you get the appointment, arrange to qualify the buyers in their home, if possible.

Do not give out the address.

Never show properties in separate cars.

1:00-2:00   Lunch

2:00-3:00   Review your latest MLS book for new listings. Call your buying prospects for an appointment to see appropriate homes. "Prioritize" your prospects by need and ability to buy. The best way to keep up is to set a time each week to review new listings. Spread out the prospect cards and arrange them in price order. Find at least one new property for each, if possible, and WITHOUT FAIL contact each prospect at least once a week.

3:00-5:00   Catch-up time. My free time was used as follows:

_____

5:00-6:00   Supper with your family.

6:00-7:00   Return to the office and call 10 of the homeowners listed below to whom you mailed "Notice of Listing" cards on Tuesday.

For an example of what to say, see Page A-7.

Record of "Notice of Listing" Cards

*Call these first

Name	Street Address	Phone	Comments
*			
*			
*			
*			
*			
*			
*			
*			
*			
*			

7:00-8:00   Read "How to List and Sell Real Estate".

Daily Summary

I have attained my goal for Thursday by: Yes   No

    Taking Floor Duty after adequate preparation;   _____   _____

    Calling my buying prospects about new listings;   _____   _____

    Catching up on uncompleted tasks;   _____   _____

    Calling 10 owners of Notice of Listing .cards;   _____   _____

    Reading for one hour on a real estate subject;   _____   _____

    Putting unfinished items on next day's agenda;   _____   _____

    Having a good day.   _____   _____

Comments or questions: _____

_____

_____

_____

Today I Developed the Following Prospects:

Name	Phone	Address	Buyer Seller	Source

$$$

I am Totally Committed to My Success!

Day Twenty-Six

FRIDAY

8:30-9:00   Discuss your progress with your Broker. This is the time to talk about whether you feel good about your work to date, and the things you most like to work on.

9:00-11:00   Continue preparing for your "Open House" Sunday by preparing small poster board cards to call attention to the benefits of the home. ("Water heater is less than 3 years old"--"Be sure not to miss this large walk-in closet"--etc.) The most pleasing colors seem to be beige stock with dark green or dark blue marker. Ask the listing salesman to help you prepare financing alternatives to show prospects.

11:00-12:00   Free time. Also a good time to get the car washed.

12:00-1:30   Lunch. While out at lunch; stop at an office supply store to get a guest book for your Open House.

1:30-4:00   Prepare a handout sheet to be given at your open house. For an example of what to put in it, see Page A-32. Make 20 copies and place them with your other items for Sunday. Get enough Open House signs from the storeroom for Sunday. Put them in your car with the rest of the supplies.

4:00-5:00   Free time - catch up if you've fallen behind.

Daily Summary

I have attained my goal for Friday by: Yes   No

Discussing my progress with my broker;   _____   _____

Preparing poster cards for my Open House;   _____   _____

Catching up - washing car, etc.;   _____   _____

Purchasing a guest book for my open house;   _____   _____

Preparing a handout sheet for Open House;   _____   _____

Putting unfinished items on next day's agenda;   _____   _____

Having a good day.   _____   _____

Comments or questions: _____

_____

_____

_____

Today I Developed the Following Prospects:

Name	Phone	Address	Buyer Seller	Source
_____	_____	_____	_____	_____
_____	_____	_____	_____	_____
_____	_____	_____	_____	_____

$$

I am Totally Committed to My Success!

Day Twenty-Seven

SATURDAY

9:00-10:00 Prepare handout package for 20 homeowners in your farm area to whom you mailed letters on Wednesday. Attach your business card to a simple gift like a company pen, note pads or a refrigerator magnet.

10:00-12:00 Visit 20 homeowners in your farm area. For an example of what to say, see Page A-27 Try to complete a Homeowner's Information sheet for each property, but if owner is reluctant, don't push.

Record of Farm Area Visits

Name	Address	Phone	Comments

12:00-1:00   Call on 10 of the 20 Notice of Listing cards you mailed on Wednesday. For an example of what to say, see Page A-7.

Record of "Notice of Listing" Cards
*Call these first

Name	Street Address	Phone	Comments
* _____	_____	_____	_____
_____	_____	_____	_____
* _____	_____	_____	_____
_____	_____	_____	_____
* _____	_____	_____	_____
_____	_____	_____	_____
* _____	_____	_____	_____
_____	_____	_____	_____
* _____	_____	_____	_____
_____	_____	_____	_____
* _____	_____	_____	_____
_____	_____	_____	_____
* _____	_____	_____	_____
_____	_____	_____	_____
* _____	_____	_____	_____
_____	_____	_____	_____
* _____	_____	_____	_____
_____	_____	_____	_____
* _____	_____	_____	_____
_____	_____	_____	_____
* _____	_____	_____	_____
_____	_____	_____	_____

Daily Summary

I have attained my goal for Saturday by:	Yes	No
Preparing handout package for my farm area;	_____	_____
Visiting 20 homeowners in my farm area;	_____	_____
Calling on 10 Notice of Listing cards;	_____	_____
Having a good day.	_____	_____

Comments or questions: _____

_____

_____

_____

Today I Developed the Following Prospects:

Name	Phone	Address	Buyer Seller	Source
_____	_____	_____	_____	_____
_____	_____	_____	_____	_____
_____	_____	_____	_____	_____
_____	_____	_____	_____	_____

$$$

I am Totally Committed to My Success!

Day Twenty-Eight

SUNDAY

11:00-12:00   Eat a hearty lunch and dress professionally for your open house.

12:00-1:00   Get everything packed in your car for the afternoon.
          Open House signs
          Guest Book
          Poster cards
          Prospect cards
          Comparable properties
          Business cards
          Giveaways
          Financing alternatives
          "How to List and Sell Real Estate" by Danielle Kennedy

2:00-5:00   Open House.
Greet every guest pleasantly.
"Demonstrate" the property, showing every favorable feature.
Discuss the financing alternatives with interested prospects.
Ask questions of those not interested. Turn them into prospects for another property.

Comments or questions: _____

_____

_____

_____

Today I Developed the Following Prospects:

Name	Phone	Address	Buyer Seller	Source

$$$

I am Totally Committed to My Success!

Day Twenty-Nine

MONDAY

8:30-9:00 Get to work early and get organized for the new week.

9:00-10:00 Attend sales meeting or review transactions for last week. Plan the route for inspecting new listings.

10:00-12:00 Inspect new listings to keep you informed.

12:00-1:00 Lunch

1:00-3:00 Plan the balance of this book on your own. We have provided a planning guide for each day of this week through Saturday. Go over your plan at 9:30 am tomorrow with your broker.

Plan the balance of today:

Time:	Action:
3:00	
3:30	
4:00	
4:30	
5:00	
5:30	
6:00	
6:30	
7:00	
7:30	

Today I Developed the Following Prospects:

Name	Phone	Address	Buyer Seller	Source

$$

I am Totally Committed to My Success!

Day Thirty

TUESDAY

This is your thirtieth day in the real estate business.

If you have completed all the tasks set forth in this book you have been quite productive, and may have several good buying or selling prospects.

While the first 30 days are crucial to ensuring a good start, the next six months will determine whether you have embarked on a career, or just had a brief visit to a different job.

Real Estate is hard work.

Real Estate is organization and planning.

Real Estate is prospecting.

Real Estate can be the most enjoyable, high paying work available, but you must treat it seriously.

If you experience "valleys" in your production, come home to this book, and "get back to the basics."

Tuesday:

Time: **Action:**

8:30   _____

9:00   _____

9:30   _____

10:00 _____

10:30 _____

11:00 _____

11:30 _____

12:00 _____

12:30 _____

1:00   _____

1:30 _____

2:00 _____

2:30 _____

3:00 _____

3:30 _____

4:00 _____

4:30 _____

5:00 _____

5:30 _____

6:00 _____

6:30 _____

7:00 _____

7:30 _____

8:00 _____

8:30 _____

Comments or questions: _____

_____

_____

Today I Developed the Following Prospects:

Name	Phone	Address	Buyer Seller	Source

$$$

I am Totally Committed to My Success!

ADDENDUM
Table of Contents

A-1

Introduction to Friends Concerning Your New Career in Real Estate

(Notecard Format)

Rita Santamaria is pleased to announce her association with Champions Realty as a licensed real estate professional specializing in the northwest area of the city. I am asking for your help. If you or if anyone you know, has a real estate need either to buy or sell a home, please give me a call.

Enclosed is my business card, in fact I have a few extras, please hand them out to anyone that might be able to use my services.

Thank you for your help ahead of time. I promise that I will take good care of you or anyone that you send my way.

Sincerely,
Rita Santamaria

YOU NEED
YOUR NAME HERE

Your Name Here
Title
Title
Title

Whether you're looking for a home to buy or planning to sell your present one, you deserve the help of a trained, experienced and dedicated real estate professional such as myself.

I will be pleased to provide you with a full range of real estate services. I have both knowledge of the local market, as well as access to both local and nationwide networks of real estate experts. You can be sure I will be able to help you locate the ideal property or help you find that "dream house."

If you're thinking of making a move, put a real estate expert to work for you. Please drop by my office or give me a call today.

ADDITIONAL TITLE OR AWARD
ADDITIONAL TITLE OR AWARD
ADDITIONAL TITLE OR AWARD
ADDITIONAL TITLE OR AWARD

PLEASE GIVE
ME A CALL

YOUR LOGO HERE

123 ANYTOWN STREET
ANYTOWN, USA

BUSINESS PHONE (000) 000-0000
RES. PHONE (000) 000-0000
FAX PHONE (000) 000-0000

A-2

Follow-Up Phone Call to Friends
Whom You Sent Announcement Cards To

Hi, Jim, this is Rita Santamaria. How are you? I was calling to see if you received my card last week announcing my new career and recent affiliation with Champions Realty? I really need your help Jim. I know over the years that you and Martha have been very good friends and have helped me in so many ways. I know that every time I have a chance to mention a good CPA to someone, I tell them to use Jim McCullough. Here is how you can help me. If you know of anyone or hear of anyone who has a need to purchase a home, sell property, or buy property, they need to call me. I am relying on my friends to help me out with this new endeavor. I am excited about the opportunity available to me in our real estate market. I assure you, anyone you send my way, I will take very good care of. I know that people I send to you are always satisfied with the exceptional service you give them. Do you know of anyone right now I might call? I want to thank you for your referrals ahead of time and let's get together soon for lunch.

Thank you.

! Remember: Ask 20 people each day:
   " Who do you know that wants to buy or sell real estate?"

Follow Up!

A-3

Follow Up Phone Call to People Whom You Sent Congratulatory Cards To

(Newlyweds, Births, & Career Promotions)

Hello, is this Sharon Willhelm? This is Rita Santamaria. I'm the real estate agent who sent you the extra clipping about your job promotion. Congratulations again. Do you have just a moment? I'd like to talk to you about your real estate needs. Do you own your own home? Does the size of your home fit your current family needs? I have a number of properties that range from single-family homes to townhomes and high-rises. If by chance you are considering making a change of life-style by house size, either larger or smaller, I would like the opportunity to work with you. Would it be acceptable for me to send you some information about my company and myself? Would you also like for me to put some flyers in the envelope showing townhomes, high-rises, and single-family dwellings in any particular part of town? Then, I will put in some current information on high rises, since you have some interest in that particular type of home, and after browsing through those if you find some that you like, just give me a call and I will be happy to show you any of those properties.

Thank you for your time and again congratulations on your new job promotion.

A-4

For Rent by Owner
What to Say when Cold Calling

(Agent will obtain actual name from Cole's Directory.)

Mr. Homeowner, this is Rita Santamaria from Champions Realty. I lease properties in your neighborhood. Right now we have an inventory of people needing to rent. Would you allow myself and agents from our company to lease your property? My company charges first month I s rent as our leasing fee. Is that agreeable with you? Mr. Homeowner, without any additional charge, we can screen potential tenants, make appointments, advertise and do the paperwork for you by simply listing your rental property with our firm. We can take this job off your list of "to-do's" and all for a 1-month rental fee when we lease it for you. And, as I mentioned earlier, our lease market is very active at Champions Realty. May I come by tonight between 6 & 7pm or would this afternoon at 4pm be better?

Thank you. I'll see you at 4pm.

A-5

Notice of Listing

(Note card Format)

Rita Santamaria and Champions Realty have recently listed a home in your neighborhood at 156 Sandstone. If you know of anyone who would like to move into our neighborhood, please have them give me a call at Champions Realty, 893-4484.

The house will be held open for the general public to view on Sunday, November 14, 20_ _ from 2 to 5 PM in the afternoon.

Thank you very much.

Your neighborhood real estate specialist,
Rita Santamaria

A-6

Homework is my business.

Return this card today and I'll help with yours

I would like more information on the services you offer.

I'm interested in:

☐ Buying a home   ☐ Financing
☐ Selling a home   ☐ Investment properties
☐ A market analysis   ☐ Other _____
    of my home

_____   _____
Name   Home Phone

_____   _____
Office Phone   Best Time to Call

If your property is now listed for sale or lease, this is
not intended as a solicitation of that listing.
© The Austin Group Ltd. 1990   © Travis Evans / Unicom Photos. All rights reserved.

Agent Name
Company Name
Company Address
Company City, ST ZIP

PRESORTED
FIRST-CLASS
MAIL
U.S. POSTAGE
PAID
TAG

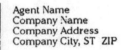

Homework is my business
JUST LISTED

Homeowner Name
Homeowner Address
Homeowner City, ST ZIP

A-7

Prospecting Around a Listing on the Phone
To Homeowners in Your Farm Area

(Ring, Ring)

Agent - Hello, My name is Rita Santamaria, I'm a real estate specialist living in your neighborhood and associated with Champions Realty. I hope you've seen our office at the front of your neighborhood. I'm just calling tonight to let you know I have recently listed a house just three doors down from yours on Bitter Sweet Court. The listing price is $118,000. Do you know anyone who might want to see it? I will be happy to make an appointment with the homeowner and show the house to any friends that you may have. Is there any real estate need that I can help you with? If you are curious about the market value of your property or the homes in Fair Valley, I would be happy to drop by a personalized market analysis and explain to you how our properties have in fact appreciated overt the last couple of years in Fair Valley. Do you have a real estate need at this time? Do you know of anyone who might want to look at my listings in Fair Valley? Again, my name is Rita Santamaria and I live just about 2 blocks over. I don't expect this house to stay on the market very long. It's priced to sell and shows well.

Again, thank you for your time. Good-bye.

A-8

Notice of Sale

(Note card Format)

Rita Santamaria & Champions Realty is excited to announce the sale of a home in your neighborhood at 126 Sandstone Dr. The new neighbors will be moving in soon. Please make them feel welcome.

If you have a friend you would like to move into our neighborhood, have them give me a call, Rita Santamaria. The agent who gets the job done in the shortest amount of time, with the most benefit to you, the homeowner.

Rita Santamaria
Champions Realty
893-4484

A-9

Notice of Sale Cards
What to Say for Follow Up Phone Call

(Agent will obtain actual name from Cole's Directory.)

Hello Mrs. Homeowner. This is Rita Santamaria, the real estate specialist who lives in your neighborhood. Did you receive the SOLD card I mailed to you last week? It was announcing the successful sale of Sandstone. The new owners will be moving in at the end of the month. They will be a nice addition to our neighborhood. Do you have a real estate need at this time? I rely on my friends in Fair Oaks to remember my name when they have a friend who needs to buy or sell property. Thank you ahead of time for the future business you can send my way.

Good-bye.

A-10

Cold Canvassing Your Neighborhood
What to Say to the Neighbors

Good evening, I'm Rita Santamaria, 1'm your neighbor who lives on Sunstone Dr. I walk through the neighborhood from time to time getting to meet my neighbors. I have been in real estate for about 5 years now with Champions Realty. I'm sure you've seen my signs and I know that you've gotten my information in the mail and on your front door. On a regular basis I like to let you know that I am your neighborhood specialist. If you have a real estate need, please give me a call. For your time tonight I'd like to give you these post-it notes with my name and company phone number on them. If after I leave here tonight and before I get back next time, if there is anyone that desires some type of real estate service either to purchase or sell property, please remember that is the business I am in. I am asking for your help.

Thank you for your time. Have a nice evening. Bye.

A-11

Cold Canvassing Calls

Agent will obtain actual name from Cole's Directory.

Hello, My name is Rita Santamaria; I'm a real estate agent specializing in the Fair Oaks subdivision and officing out of Champions Realty in the front of your neighborhood. Have you noticed my signs? I've been in business for a number of years and I am personally sold on the Fair Oaks neighborhood. I live here and enjoy listing properties for sale by my neighbors and also being able to bring new homeowners into our neighborhood. I'm taking some time out of my schedule today to say hello and ask you if you would be interested in my coming by and leaving a market analysis on your property to give you an idea of what values are in the Fair Oaks neighborhood today. I noticed in the Fair Oaks directory that you have a child that graduated from high school last year. Often at this time, parents are thinking about moving into something a little bit smaller, where they don't have to worry about the yard work. Would you have a need for any information on town-homes or high rises available in the area? I would be happy to drop off some of that information to you. At the same time, would you like for me to deliver to you a market analysis showing what houses just like yours have sold for in the last six months? Thank you very much. Would tonight or tomorrow night be more convenient? I have an available appointment time for tonight at 6:30 or tomorrow night at 5:00, what would be more convenient for you? O.K. I will see you tomorrow at 5:00 and again my name is Rita Santamaria, I'm with Champions Realty and I look forward to talking with you tomorrow night about condominiums that are available in this area. Do you want to stay in the school district that your children are in now, or would you be open to other parts of town? Fine, I will be happy to come by and give you information just on the northwest part of our city.

Thank you, I'll look forward to seeing you tomorrow night.

A-12

Calling Renters

Agent:

Hello my name is Rita Santamaria. I am a real estate agent specializing in selling homes in the northwest part of the city. I would like to ask you a couple of questions if you have just a moment. Is this a good time to talk with you or should I call back at a later time? (Assuming it is a good time) I notice that you are renting an apartment right now for your family. I would like to send you something in the mail to show you the tax benefits of owning rather than renting; and how over a 12-month lease, how much money you'll save, not to mention that you're building up equity in your home as well. Would that be acceptable to your Mr. Renter if I would send you information in the mail? Let me make sure that I have your address correct, that was 123 Court, Apartment 602, Houston, 77379? I will put this in the mail, and should I address this to Mr. & Mrs. John Jones? OK and thank you very much and again my name is Rita Santamaria and I am with Champions Realty; you will be getting this analysis on renting vs. owning in just a couple of days.

Thank you for your time.

A-13

Calling For Sale by Owners What to Say on the Telephone

Agent will get homeowner's name from Cole's Directory so that it will be a personal phone call.

Mr. Homeowner, I drove past your house today and saw a sign that said you want to sell your home yourself. I'm a real estate agent living in the neighborhood just 2 blocks over from your house. I specialize in the Fair Oaks subdivision and would like to send you some information which I think you will find helpful on what an agent does from the time they put the sign in the yard until the property goes to closing. You see, there's more to selling a property than just listing the property. Mr. Homeowner is there a convenient time when I could come by and drop off some information? And what I would really like to do is sit down and talk with you about the four areas that allow a house to be sold. Within these four areas, if you meet all of the criteria, there would not be any reason why your house will not sell within the next couple of months. Of course, I'm saying that based on the fact that it would be listed with an agency, because the larger percentage of homes are sold through real estate companies. And by selling it yourself, as I'm sure you recognize you're limiting the number of available prospects that would be interested in your house. Would it be convenient for me to come by this evening between 6 and 7pm?

Thank you very much; I look forward to meeting you tonight at 6:30.

Again, my name is Rita Santamaria, I'm with the Champions Realty Group and I'll see you at 6:30.

A-14

Calling on a Buyer in Person
Follow-up Call from Mailing

Agent - Hello Mr. Homeowner, I am Rita Santamaria, you received my information mailed to you just a few days ago telling you the services available through Champions Realty and myself. I would like to come in and give you information on why your house has not sold. Can I have just a moment of your time?

Homeowner invites agent into home, while sitting at the kitchen table...

Agent - Mr. Homeowner there are only 4 reasons why a house doesn't sell, or any property for that matter. Price, location, condition, and marketing plan May I explain?

You will review all aspects with homeowner.

    Is his house is in a good location?   Yes   No

    Is the condition of the house ready to be shown and sold?   Yes   No

    Price - It is priced right? If overpriced, work out a plan so that every 30 days it will be reduced by 10%.

    Marketing Plan - if everything else is in order, then go over the marketing plan & how you will personalize a plan to sell his house.

Ask for an opportunity to list & sell his house.

As shaking hands, getting ready to leave...

Most important - stop & give business card

    I want to be the one to sell your home, please give me a call, Thank You.

A-15

For Sale by Owners-Letter

February 2, 20_ _

Champions Realty
3724 FM 1960 West, #116
Anytown, TX 77069

Dear Mr. Homeowner, (you'll use your Cole's directory to get exact name)

I'm Rita Santamaria, a real estate specialist that lives in your neighborhood. You currently have your home listed for sale by owner. Many people try to sell their homes by themselves in order to save the real estate commission. I understand that in this day & time, saving money is what we are all about. My company, Champions Realty, would like to be the company you choose to list your property with. Over 90% of the buyers, for residential homes, come through a real estate agent. You are missing a lot of potential buyers by not using an agent, not to mention the fact that people who come through your home are not qualified buyers. The people who come through your home with an agent are all qualified buyers, which means they are legitimate buyers. I have a track record for selling homes in your neighborhood, which is also my neighborhood. I have names you might recognize who are my satisfied customers. I would be happy to give you their phone numbers as references.

I will be dropping by your house in a couple of days and would appreciate a personal visit. I can sit down with you and tell you how we can save you time, money and get your property sold. And I believe Mr. Homeowner that is exactly what you are looking for. Thank you very much.

Sincerely yours,

A-16

Prospecting for Listings

1st Step: **The Telephone Call**

1. Call a specified number of residents each day - keep a record of calls and responses.

2. Introduce yourself and your company.

3. Make your purpose for calling clear.

4. Be friendly, yet brief.

5. Leave your name and phone number.

6. Advise of <u>future</u> call and/or visit

2nd Step: **Mail**

1. Send a handwritten note to those previously contacted by phone.

2. Thank the owner for the time spent in conversation.

3. Advise of a future visit and/or call

3rd Step: **Personal Visit**

1. Visit those previously contacted by phone and/or mail.

2. Present a friendly attitude of visiting, instead of soliciting

3. Introduce yourself and your Company and offer your business card

4. Remind owner of previous contacts and/or attempts

5. Establish that you are the area representative

6. Discuss market values in the neighborhood (a range of)

7. Do not quote a value for any property without compiling a Competitive Market Analysis

A-I7

For Sale By Owner

A. Telephone Approach

1. Introduce yourself and your company at the beginning of the conversation.

2. Suggest that you have some advice for them that concerns their selling price, showing and selling techniques, etc.

3. Make appointment to meet with both owners.

4. Be unique - ask a question, then offer your service, i.e. "How much are you asking for the property?" "I always compile a list of comparables before determining the market value."

5. Advise of future calls to check on their progress and wish them luck.

6. Be truthful and logical in your reasoning for wanting to offer help.

7. Record all calls, responses and results.

8. Follow up with a note and a visit.

B. Direct Approach

1. Introduce yourself and your company and present your card.

2. Ask about their plans for moving.

3. Ask how long the house has been on the market.

4. Ask about their advertising measures.

5. Ask their price.

6. Ask about the size of the house, i.e. number of bedrooms, baths, den, and kitchen – Reason: You want to do some research that will show how the house compares to others like it.

7. See property, if possible, and find something to be enthusiastic about.

8. Suggest that you return with this information on paper plus some advice concerning showing techniques, etc.

9. Be truthful as to your intent – you wish them luck but you want them to remember you if they tire of the selling process.

A-18

For Sale By Owner (con't)

10. Make an appointment to return with price information when both owners are present.

11. Leave card or gift (something of value – a card or a gift – but not too many things at once).

12. Advise of future contact.

Best Time to Make Cold Calls

1. When a listing has been obtained in the area.

2. When a sale has been made in the area.

3. When you have a gift item to deliver.

4. When you have new and interesting information for the residents.

5. In the afternoon or early evening.

COLD CALL RECORD EXPLANANTION

1. The street name

2. Number: The house address

   Name: The owner's name

   Telephone: The telephone number

   *Fill out an entire page before beginning your calls to save time

3. Record comments for identification purposes for your second contract. Always note someone's willingness to give you help. Follow up with a note of appreciation. A visit is sometimes even better.

A-19

For Sale By Owner (con't)

C. Direct Approach – Return Visit

1. Ask to tour property <u>again</u>.

2. Discuss various showing techniques.

3. Consult your Competitive Market Analysis for comparables.

4. Ask their plans for having home finance when sols.

5. Ask to see Deed of Trust and Note, Survey, etc.

6. Use real estate terminology when discussing finance, advertising and marketing.

7. Give general advice – not free service.

8. Repeat reasons for wanting got help.

9. Follow up with mail, phone call, and repeat visit. Then repeat process until the <u>For Sale by Owner</u> has been converted to <u>your listing</u>.

A-20

The Listing Interview

When you approach the homeowner you should plan in writing:

A. An evaluation on plain paper or lists of:
   - Properties presently on the market
   - Properties sold in the last 6 months
   - Properties that did not sell

B. Have your <u>listing kit</u> in good order.

1. <u>Be</u> <u>alert</u> for listing <u>possibilities</u> and follow-up promptly on all inquiries.

   Qualify the seller – we want properties that must be sold. (A seller that needs to sell.)

2. <u>Service</u> each listing effectively so that the seller <u>feels</u> <u>activity</u>:
   - <u>You</u> call him.
   - Send his copy of advertising.
   - Be creative.

3. Know the market so you can help prospective sellers.

4. While with your sellers, fit your personality to heirs, then:

   Stress the fact that we relieve them of the responsibility involved in the sale.

   Stress the fact that we protect them from unqualified prospects.

   Stress the fact that we make certain that an agent (licensed) is always present with a prospect when he visits the listed property.

   Stress the fact that we are ready to answer questions at any time.

   Stress the fact that we always cooperate with other realtors. (Cooperation is a privilege.)

   Stress the fact that we have a secretary to make appointments – keeps lists of such appointments – is careful with the key.

   Stress the fact that we look after the property <u>as our own</u> when the owner is out of town.

   Stress the fact that we present <u>all offers</u>.

   Stress the fact that we are a firm with a national reputation of giving quality service and a national relocation program.

A-21

The Listing Interview (con't)

Stress the fact that we have one agent completely responsible for each listing whose responsibility is to get the best possible price and terms in the least possible time with the least fuss and bother to the homeowner. The lister is completely "on the side of" the seller… but remembering that after there is fair play for both parties.

5. Through our knowledge of finance, we can present to you contracts with a loan contingency reflecting the current market, in length of time to get the interest rate attainable.

6. <u>We know our moneylenders.</u>

7. We are <u>objective</u>: We always try to avoid personal or sentimental feelings. We conduct a good negotiation.

8. Develop your own pattern. Let the real you emerge.

9. Make a good impression with your first contact. Impress the seller with the thoroughness of your inspection and procedures. Always watch your personal appearance. This will build confidence in you and your organization.

10. <u>Take plenty of time initially</u> – write in things to be excluded. Try to get them removed now – "What you see is what you get."

11. <u>Pricing Property</u>: Advise, assist and counsel – offer a range, but let the price be the seller's decision. It is his responsibility.

    Find out why that seller purchased this property. <u>Remember, there is a buyer for each and every property.</u>

12. After you have a signed listing – before you leave – start servicing the listing.

THE SUCCESSFUL SALESPERSON

List the property:

- At saleable prices
- Keeps the seller informed
- Services his listings
- Continually prospects for new listings
- Has a professional well organized listing kit
- Has an attitude of enthusiasm

A-22

Your Property   ---- Pricing To Sell

20%
Above   **1%**
$_____**FMV**_____ **of Prospects**
may buy

15%
Above   **10%**
$_____**FMV**_____ **of Prospects**
may buy

10%
Above   **25%**
$_____**FMV**_____ **of Prospects**
may buy

                                                             50%
$_____**Fair Market Value** _____ **of Prospects**
may buy

10%
Below   **75%**
$_____**FMV**_____ **of Prospects**
may buy

15%
Below   **90%**
$_____**FMV**_____ **of Prospects**
may buy

20%
Below   **99%**
$_____**FMV**_____ **of Prospects**
may buy

HOW SOON DO YOU WANT TO SELL?

A-23

FABULOUS NEW LISTING

Price...

5515 STRACK RD. #116

★ SECLUDED COMPLEX

★ TWO BEDROOMS

★ TWO & ONE-HALF BATHS

★ FORMAL DINING ROOM

★ TWO LIVING AREAS

★ HIGH CEILINGS THRU'OUT

★ ATTACHED GARAGE

★ MAINTENANCE-FREE LIVING

A-24

Summary of Services for Seller

You can:

1. Compare properties for current market value

2. Save seller's valuable time with professional sales force

3. Advertise in mass media

4. Illustrate property to 95% of area real estate agents – MLS

5. Qualify the buyer

6. Present marketing features for the buyer

7. Give confidence to buyer

8. "Close" at the time of greatest interest

9. Provide personal and financial protection

10. Prepare contract, keeping owner's interest expressed

11. Present and negotiate contract with impersonal reflection

12. Prepare closing cost estimate showing seller's net

13. Assist buyer in securing financing

14. Follow-up with buyer's responsibilities

15. Interpret closing conditions

16. Care for property in absence of owner

17. Service buyers transferring here from out-of-town who naturally go through Realtor firms – because of limited time, lack of knowledge of city

18. Promote property by calling other Realtors

19. Hold a Realtor open house

20. Hold a public open house

21. Record all showings and responses

22. Make a weekly progress report

A-25

Quick Property List

STREET	ADDRESS	BEDS	BATHS	SQFT	LISTPRICE	SOLDDATE	DOM
ACTIVES							
5515	STRACK ROAD		2/1	1500	$92,500		
5515	STRACK RD		2/1	1500	$89,900		
5515	STRACK		2/1	1219	$75,000		
PENDINGS							
5515	STRACK #133	1/	1/1	1004	$58,900		181
AVERAGES:		1.8	1.75	1306	$79,075		181
SOLDS							
5515	STRACK RD	2/	2/1	−1500	$86,500	04/06/94	113
5515	STRACK RD	3/	2/5	1500	$86,500	12/16/92	59
5515	STRACK	2/	2/1	1219	$83,000	03/16/94	60
5515	STRACK RD	1/	1/1	1004	$56,900	12/31/92	238
AVERAGES:		2.0	1.75	1306	$78,225		118

Summary Of
Properties Sold Analysis

Address	List Price	Sold Price	DOM	%CHG	Sold Price/SqFt
5515 Strack Rd #	$86,500.00	$85,000.00	113	-1.7%	$56.67
5515 Strack Rd #	$86,500.00	$84,000.00	59	-2.9%	$56.00
5515 Strack #	$83,000.00	$77,500.00	60	-6.6%	$63.58
5515 Strack Rd #	$56,900.00	$49,500.00	238	-13.0%	$49.30
Tot. Averages:	**$78,225**	**$74,000.**	**118**	**-5.4%**	**$56**

A-26

A Letter to Your Farm Area

Dear John & Mary Jones,

I am a neighbor of yours and live with around the corner on <u>Sunstone</u>. My name is Rita Santamaria.

My full-time job is real estate brokerage services, specializing in <u>Friendly Oaks</u>.

I am asking for your help. If you have a real estate need, either to buy another property, or sell one that you currently own, please call me. Also, your are an acting community leader and interface with a lot of people. If any of your friends have a real estate need, please give my name to them as well.

Enclosed are my business cards, please pass them out.

Sincerely,

P.S. I hope to personally see you soon.

A-27

Personal Visit to Homeowner to Whom You Previously Mailed a Letter

Agent - Hello, I'm Rita Santamaria with Champions Realty. I mailed a letter to you a few days ago telling you about our company. You may remember in the letter, I told you I specialize in this neighborhood.

Neighbor Responds

Agent - I was hoping you could help me. Do you know of anyone who might want to move to our neighborhood?

Neighbor Responds

Agent - If you have a real estate need, or if you hear of someone who wants to buy or sell, please give them my card. I promise to do a good job helping them - or you. Here's a free gift for your time.

Thank You.

TIPS TO THE SELLER

LET YOUR HOME SMILE A WELCOME TO BUYERS

1. First impressions are lasting. The front door greets the prospect. Make sure it is fresh, clean, and scrubbed looking. Keep lawn trimmed and edged and the yard free of refuse.

2. Decorate for a quick sale. Faded walls and worn woodwork reduce appeal. Why try to tell the prospect how your home could look, when you can show him by redecorating? A quicker sale at a higher price will result. An investment in new kitchen wallpaper will pay dividends.

3. Let the sun shine in. Open draperies and curtains and let the prospect see how cheerful your home can be. (Dark rooms do not appeal.)

4. Fix that faucet! Dripping water discolors sinks and suggests faulty plumbing.

5. Repairs can make a big difference. Loose knobs, sticking doors and windows, warped cabinet drawers and other minor flaws detract from home value.

6. From top to bottom. Display the full value of your attic and other utility space by removing all unnecessary articles.

7. Safety first. Keep stairways clear. Avoid cluttered appearances and possible injuries.

8. Make closets look bigger. Neat well-ordered closets show that pace is ample.

9. Bathrooms help sell homes. Check and repair caulking in bathtubs and showers. Make this room sparkle.

10. Arrange bedrooms neatly. Remove excess furniture. Use attractive bedspreads and freshly laundered curtains.

11. Can you see the light? Illumination is like a welcome sign. The potential buyer will feel a glowing warmth when you turn on all your lights for an evening inspection.

WHEN THE AGENT SHOWS THE HOUSE

12. Three's a crowd. Avoid having too many people present during inspections. The potential buyer will feel like an intruder and will hurry through the house.

13. Music is mellow. But not when showing the house. Turn off the blaring radio or television. Let the salesman and buyer talk free of disturbances.

14. Pets underfoot? Keep them out of the way-preferably out of the house.

15. Silence is golden. Be courteous but don't force conversation with the potential buyer. He wants to inspect your house – not pay a social call.

16. Be it ever so humble. Never apologize for the appearance of your home. After all, it has been lived in. Let the trained salesman answer any objections. This is his job.

17. In the background. The salesman knows the buyers requirements and can better emphasize the features of your home when you don't tag along. You will be called if needed.

18. Why put the cart before the horse? Trying to dispose of furniture and furnishings to the potential buyer before he has purchased the house often loses the sale.

19. A word to the wise. Let your Realtor discuss price terms, possession and other factors with the customer. He is eminently qualified to bring negotiations to a favorable conclusion.

20. Use your agent. Show your home to prospective customers only by appointment through your agent. Your cooperation will be appreciated an will help close the sale more quickly.

A-29

Calling Expired Listings

Ring Ring - Hello

Agent - Hello Mrs. Smith, this is Rita Santamaria, a neighbor on Sunstone.

I am calling my neighbors today to say hello and to let you know I sell the Friendly Oaks subdivision.

I am with Champions Real Estate and our office is right in front of the neighborhood. Have you seen it?

If you would like a free market analysis on your home or need a speaker for any clubs you belong to, I would be happy to talk about the "sales process", from contract to closing, or any related real estate topic, within my area of expertise.

Do you have a real estate need that I might be able to help you with today?

May I send you some of my business cards? If you have a friend who needs an agent please tell them about me.

Thank you for your time.

I'll be keeping in touch with you.

A-30

Questions to Ask Ad Callers

Controlling the Conversation

When answering an ad call, the person who is asking all of the questions is the one who is in charge and is controlling the conversation. What you want to do, as a salesperson, is not to give just all of the answers, but also to be gaining information from that prospect. The one who takes control of the prospect is the one who will end up working with them.

The following are a list of questions that will help you in controlling the ad call.

1.   Is this the area of town that you want to live in?
2.   Have you been qualified?
3.   Is this the price range that you are qualified to purchase in?
4.   What is the distance to work that you are willing to drive?
5.   What school district do you want to live in?
6.   Is there one style home that you prefer over another?
7.   Is living in a neighborhood that has area tennis courts & swimming pool important to you?
8.   How many bedrooms, how many baths do you need?
9.   Have you been working with any other agents?
10.   What motivated you to pick up the phone and call our company?
    ♦   Was it the location of the neighborhood?
    ♦   Was it the outside features/style of the home?
    ♦   Was it the way the ad was written?
11.   How long have you been looking for a home?
12.   Are you currently under lease?
13.   How much money do you have to invest in a home? Is this money including the down payment & closing cost
14.   If we were to find a home today, would you be able to follow through and start the paperwork right away?
15.   Is there anything that would keep you from moving into a house in 45 days?
16.   Do you have another house to sell?

A-31

Prospect Card File

Howard, Jeff J.   1906 N. Margo
                                         334-3432
                                         Wife – Evelyn
                                         No children

3/28 Referred by J. Scott
4/18 Bought 1906 N. Margo
6/1   Deal closed – Sent thank-you card
7/3   Follow-up call – O. K.
12/20 Christmas card & call
4/2   1 year card

Howard, Jeff J.   Card #2

4/6   Call – May be transferred in August
6/1   Call – Listing presentation
7/20 House V/c – Close 9/1/77
7/22 Referred to Jones Co. in Tucson
9/1   House closed
9/3   Thank-you card to new address in Tucson
10/16 Referral check from Tucson broker

NAME_____

TELEPHONE_____ PURCHASE_
RENT ___

TYPE OF HOUSING DESIRED: ____single family ____2-family ____apartment
____condominium ____ranch ____split level ____ 2-story
____contemporary ____traditional ____spanish ____victorian
No. rooms _____ Bedrooms _____ Baths _____ Price limits $_____to $_____
Subdivision or Area preferred _____ Down payment $_____
School District preferred _____ Mo. Payment $_____
Type and amount of financing preferred _____
Want occupancy by _____19___.

PRESENT HOUSING DATA:

Address _____ City _____State_____
Type and size_____ No. rooms_____ Bedrooms____baths_____
Rent?_____Mo. rent $_____ Lease expires _____ 19___.
Own? _____Mo. pymt.$_____ plan to sell by _____ 19___.

EMPLOYMENT INFORMATION

Place of work _____ Occupation _____
How long employed?_____ Present Mo. salary $_____Business ph._____
Place of Spouse's employment_____ Mo. salary $_____
Any overtime or other income? _____ Amount $_____
Total mo. family income $_____

FOR PURCHASE APPLICANTS ONLY:

Current mortgage obligation $_____ Mo. payment $_____ Taxes $___
Other installment loans $_____ Mo. payments$_____
Totals . . . . $_____ $_____

PERSONAL REFERENCES:

Bank: Checking Account at _____ Savings Account at _____
Store: Charge Account at _____ Others _____
Personal:_____

_____
(Signature of Applicant)

A-32

REALTORS OPEN HOUSE

12007 KLEINMEADOW DRIVE

KLEINBROOK SUBDIVISION

MLS#285832 $94,900

WEDNESDAY, FEBRUARY 21ST

11:30 A.M. - 2:00 P.M.

CATERED LUNCH BY JAMI EDABURN-SMITH
Fresh Salsa With Tostado Chips
King Ranch Chicken or Mini Tacos
Spanish Style Rice
Fresh Fruit Tray

♥♥♥♥♥♥♥♥♥♥♥♥♥♥♥♥♥♥♥♥♥♥♥♥♥♥♥♥♥♥♥♥♥

BEAUTIFUL NEW HOME BUILT AS A MODEL
WITH MANY EXTRAS!
OVERSIZED MASTER BEDROOM WITH ENORMOUS
WALK-IN CLOSET!
BUILT-IN DESK/WORK STATION IN 2ND BEDROOM
TILED FIREPLACE!
ENORMOUS PANTRY WITH ATTACHED LAUNDRY ROOM
SPACIOUS BACK YARD!

♥♥♥♥♥♥♥♥♥

PROUDLY PRESENTED BY

REDUCED!!

$207,500
TO
$199,900

MLS# 277134

6026 Coral Ridge
Champions South
A WONDERFUL HOME!

View of 3rd green, Jackrabbit Champions

Open plan shows light and bright

Courtyard entry

Nice neutral colors

Wall of windows overlooking course

Updating includes roof, tile, carpet

paint and some papers

For more information call listing agent

A-33

THE MARKET REPORT

GREENWOOD FOREST

January

THE MARKET REPORT is an informational service of
The chart below indicates by price range the number of homes for sale and represents the **SELLER SUPPLY** as of the first of the month.

PRICE RANGE	Jan	Feb	Mar	Apr	May	Jun	Jul	Aug	Sep	Oct	Nov	Dec
NUMBER OF CURRENT LISTINGS												
BELOW 99,999	4											
100,000 - 114,999	5											
115,000 - 129,999	7											
130,000 - 139,999	6											
140,000 - 149,999												
150,000 - 159,999												
160,000 - 169,999												
170,000 - 179,999	1											
189,000 - 199,999	1											
200,000 - 299,999	4											
300,000 - 399,999	1											
400,000 - 499,999												
500,000 & ABOVE	1											
TOTALS:	30											

The Average Sale Price in December was $116,000.

The List to Sale Price Ratio was 94%.

BUYER DEMAND of the market as recorded by REALTORS each month is depicted below. Buyer demand represents home purchases **INITIATED** in the months recorded and is expressed in the **LIST PRICE** of the home.

PRICE RANGE	Jan	Feb	Mar	Apr	May	Jun	Jul	Aug	Sep	Oct	Nov	Dec	TOTALS
MONTHLY SALES													
BELOW 99,999	1	1		2		1	3	1		2	1		12
100,000 - 114,999			1			2							3
115,000 - 129,999		2		4	2	4	1	3	1	2	2	1	22
130,000 - 139,999			1				1	2	1				5
140,000 - 149,999		1	2			1		1					5
150,000 - 159,999							1						1
160,000 - 169,999			1		1								2
170,000 - 179,999													
180,000 - 199,999						1							1
200,000 - 299,999													
300,000 - 399,999													
400,000 - 499,999													
500,000 & ABOVE													
TOTALS	1	4	4	7	3	9	6	7	2	4	3	1	51

A-34

Thank You Letter to Homeowner in Farm Area

Thanking them for allowing you to have personal visit with them

(Notecard format)

Dear Mary & John:

Thank you for your time last Tuesday night. It was my pleasure getting to meet you. I look forward to seeing you on a more regular basis. Again, I am asking for your help. If you know of anyone who might be able to use my services as a real estate professional specializing in the northwest area of town, please give them my business card. I have enclosed a few extras hoping that you will pass them on to a friend who may need my real estate services.

Thank you very much.

You neighbor,
Rita Santamaria
Champions Realty

A-35

A-35
NAME
Title
Title
Title
Res. (000) 000-0000

HOMEOWNERS UPDATE

VOLUME 13, NUMBER 8

Purchasing Your Dream Home

I t's an exciting feeling to turn the key and unlock the door of your new home. Whether you've bought several homes or only one, the choices today might seem overwhelming at first. But if you follow a few simple guidelines, your home purchase could turn out to be much easier than expected.

❖ First, you need to consider your finances. How much can you afford to spend? A general rule of thumb is you should spend approximately 29 percent of your monthly gross income on housing, including mortgage payments, taxes and insurance premiums.

❖ Next, consider your housing options. Do you want a new or existing home, a custom-built home or a condominium? Do you want a large back yard? What about the size of the kitchen? Do you want

Consider your personal preferences, goals and lifestyle when shopping for a new home.

carpet throughout the house? You need to ask yourself these questions as well as how many bedrooms and bathrooms you will need and want.

❖ Then determine the area that best fits your needs regarding distance and access to work, schools, recreational facilities, shopping, and other necessities.

❖ Once you decide on the area you like best, compare the layout and size of different neighborhood homes. It is often helpful to keep notes on each house you like. Jot down information such as address, price, financing, taxes, age and style of house, lot size, number of bedrooms and baths, dislikes, distance to work, etc.

I would be happy to help you find your dream home. Just give me a call!

A-36

Step #1: For <u>thirty days</u> first thing in the morning, last thing at night, by yourself, in front of a mirror, stand up straight, square your shoulders, look yourself in the eye and quietly, firmly say in the first-person, present-tense:

> "I, _____, am a person of integrity with a good attitude and specific goals. I have a high energy level, am enthusiastic, and take pride in my appearance and what I do. I have a sense of humor, lots of faith, wisdom, and the vision, empathy and courage to use my talents effectively. I have character and am knowledgeable. My convictions are strong and I have a healthy self-image, a passion for what is right and a solid hope for the future.
>
> I am an honest, sincere, hard-working person. I am tough but fair and sensitive. I'm disciplined, motivated, and focused. I am a good listener and patient, but take decisive action. I am bold, authoritative and confident, yet humble. I am an encourager, a good-finder, an excellent communicator and am developing winning habits. I am a student, a teacher, and a self-starter. I am obedient, loyal, responsible, dependable and prompt I have a servant's heart, am ambitious and a team player. I am personable, optimistic and organized. I am consistent, considerate and resourceful. I am intelligent, competent, persistent and creative. I am health-conscious, "balanced" and sober. I am flexible, punctual and thrifty.
>
> I am an honorable person who is truly grateful for the opportunity life has given me. These are the qualities of the winner I was born to be and I am fully committed to develop these marvelous qualities with which I have been entrusted. Tonight I'm going to sleep wonderfully well. I will dream powerful, positive dreams. I will awaken energized and refreshed, and tomorrow's going to be magnificent!"

Repeat the process the next morning and close by saying,

> "These are the qualities of the winner I was born to be. Today is the first day of the rest of my life, and it's wonderful."

After 30 days, add the next step:

Choose your strongest quality and the one you feel needs the most work.

Example: Strongest – honest. Needs most work - organized. On a separate 3x5 card, print

> "I, _____, am a completely honest person and every day I am getting better and better organized."

Do this first thing in the morning and last thing at night for one week; then repeat the process with the second strongest quality and the second one that needs the most work. Do this until you've completed the entire list. This process will change your life for the better.

NOTE: Keep this handy and use it regularly for the rest of your life!

I. GUIDELINES FOR NEGOTIATING THE CONTRACT

1. KEEP PERSONALITIES OUT
    It is not in anyone's best interest to try and "get the best of" anybody

2. NEGOTIATE THE DIFFERENCES
    Avoid reopening points already agreed upon

3. CENTER IN ONE REAL NEEDS
    What is in the best interest of your customer?
    Which of the following are critical to each party?
    > Price
    > Possession date
    > Personal property
    > Terms

4. CONCENTRATE ON THIS OFFER
    Don't let the customer stray away from here and now

5. SPLIT THE DIFFERENCES
    Keep it balanced

6. MAINTAIN A POSITIVE APPROACH
    KEEP YOUR COOL!!

II. AGENT PREPARATION

1. Thank agent for offer
2. Go over offer in detail
3. Do not offer "presumed" responses
4. Keep the other agent informed
5. Keep personalities out of the negotiating

III. PRESENTATION

1. Verbally present acceptable term (Per listing agreement)
2. Give buyer's reasons for wanting to buy seller's property
3. Present written offer
4. Present estimates of proceeds

BUYING SIGNALS:

1. Re-examine the property - "Can we go back to...?"
2. Assume mental ownership - "Bobby can have the small bedroom."
              "The sofa would fit right here."
3. Request specific details - "What is the monthly payment on this one?"
4. Start negotiating for a concession - "Do you think the drapes will stay'
5. Seek reassurance - "This is really a nice area, isn't it?"
6. Exhibit change in behavior, either positive or negative.
7. Start to sell the other party - "Alice, you would love this kitchen!"
8. Closely examine the contract - "What does this section mean?"
9. Ask about the next step - "What do we have to do now?"

TYPES OF CLOSINGS:

1. **Urgency** - use only when true
2. **Minor point** - The either/or approach
3. **Stair-Step** - One little step at a time
4. **Rita's Closing** - Use the wastebasket!
5. **Advisory** - Use the outside expert
6. **Assumptive** - Not if, but when
7. **Ben Franklin Close**
8. **Ask them to buy** - When all else fails

READING LIST

THE TIME TRAP - MACKENZIE

SECRETS OF CLOSING THE SALE - ZIG ZIGLAR

HOW TO STOPWORRYING AND START LIVING - DALE CARNEGIE

THE PSYCHOLOGY OF WINNING - DENNIS WAITLEY

THE RICHEST MAN IN BABYLON - GEORGE CLESON

HOW TO MASTER THE ART OF SELLING - TOM HOPKINS

PSYCHOCYBERNETICS - MATTHEW MALTZ

SEVEN HABITS OF SUCCESSFUL PEOPLE - STEVEN COVEY

WORLD'S GREATEST SALESMAN - OG MANDINO

POWER OF POSITIVE THINGS - EZRA T. BENTZEN

ABOUT THE AUTHOR

Rita Santamaria is celebrating 20 years as founder and owner of Champions School of Real Estate. With offices currently in Houston and Dallas, Texas, she plans on opening a new third location soon in northwest Dallas.

Some of her most recent achievements include:
— Houston WCR FM 1960 Chapter President
— The Montgomery County Association of REALTORS® "Affiliate of the Year"
— The Houston WCR chapter "Educator of the Year"

In 2002, she was recognized by the Northwest Harris County Forum of business owners in Houston, TX as the "Outstanding Community Leader of the Year."

Rita Santamaria and Champions School were the 2002 Texas Statewide WCR "Affiliate of the Year." In 2002 she received the 5.0 Club Award for outstanding teaching performance from the RealtyU national consortium of schools.

Having had over ten real estate textbooks published, and used by over 25,000 students annually, her most popular book on how to get started in your real estate career, *30 Days to Success*, is published by South-Western Publishing, a Thomson Company.

Rita grew up in south Florida and graduated from Florida State University with a Bachelor's of Science degree. She is married to Henry, a commercial broker, and together they have five children.

Notes

Notes

Notes

Notes

Notes

Notes

Notes

Notes

Luther refused to attribute any saving power to the natural orders. They are so completely involved in sin that they actually tend to hide rather than reveal the saving will of God. However, he considers them the practical realm of social ethics. They alone apply to all men regardless of their relationship to the Cross, for they alone are understandable to the unregenerate man. Since, according to Luther, the Christians constitute only a small minority among the nations of the world, practical norms for society cannot be norms that are meaningful to Christians alone.[92] For this reason, God deals with the Christians through His means of grace, the Word, and the Sacraments, but He deals with men in general through the natural orders as they shape nature and history.[93] Here God's preserving and punishing

. . . .

there, and face all the other troubles and worries of the married life? Am I supposed to be a prisoner of marriage?' Oh, you poor miserable man, you have taken a wife, tsk, tsk, so much trouble and worry! It is better to remain single and to live a quiet life without care. I shall become a priest or a nun and tell my children to do the same."

[92] W.A., 52, 291, 3 (Hauspostille, 1544): "What is sin? Is it to steal, to murder, to commit adultery, and the like? These are indeed sins, but they are not the true chief sins. Many persons are not guilty of these manifest sins; but of that chief sin of which the Holy Spirit reproves the world—no one is free, else the Holy Spirit could not reprove the whole world. This great sin is the unbelief of the world, the refusal to believe in Jesus Christ. Nor does the world know anything of this sin before the Holy Spirit reproves the people of it through His teachings; the world considers only such deeds sinful as are contrary to the second table of the Law. It knows nothing of Christ, and much less is it aware of the sin of not believing in Him. . . . The Holy Spirit, therefore, preaches this truth that all men without exception are sinners and cannot of themselves believe in Christ. This is, of course, strange preaching for the world. The world of itself is perfectly ignorant of the duty of having faith in the man Jesus."

[93] W.A., 25, 141, 25 (Lectures on Isaiah, 1527-29, 1532-34):

power can be seen by all.[94]

In summary, it can be said that the practical principle of Luther's social ethics is his concept of the natural orders. He describes them as being divinely ordained and having their source in the preserving will of God. Thus they help to maintain the world until the day of Jesus Christ. However, they are also of an emergency character. In their present form, the family, secular authority, and all the human callings within society are means of directing the creative energy of man, which as a result of sin could easily destroy him, into constructive channels. Marriage and the family make sexual chastity possible. Though at first ordained by God as a means of service, marriage became as a result of sin also the divine remedy against the disease of lust.[95] Authority is also a divine order which precedes the Fall.[96]

. . . .

"As a theological proposition, this passage deals with power; God claims all power; all kingdoms are established and maintained by God. He says: 'I have commanded my consecrated ones.' This passage serves to confirm Romans 13 against seditionists, showing that it is simply not permitted to resist the powers, unless it is done because of a new order and mandate from God." See also Phila. Ed., I, 265: "Therefore, it would be most profitable for rulers, that they read, or have read to them, from youth on, the histories, both in sacred and in profane books, in which they would find more examples and skill in ruling than in all the books of law. . . . For examples and histories benefit and teach more than the laws and statutes: there actual experience teaches, here untried and uncertain words."

[94] W.A., 50, 384, 2 (Preface to Galeatii Capellae, 1538): "History books are nothing but reports, records, and memorials to God's work and judgment. They tell how He maintains, rules, hinders, advances, punishes, and honors the world and especially mankind, giving the bad and good according to their deserts. And though there are many who neither know nor honor God, they run across these examples and historical records and begin to fear that they will experience the same fate as those who are described in these books. This has more effect on them than any

146

ethical principle of the Christian individual, faith active in love, and the divine natural law that governs the orders of nature. But Luther explains that a point of contact between the secular realm and the spiritual realm exists in the person of the individual Christian. In this point the spiritual realm penetrates the secular, without, however, abolishing it. The Gospel itself cannot be used to rule the world, because it is the Gospel and demands a voluntary response from man. It would cease to be the Gospel if it became a new law. But through the person of the believer, who is related to Christ through the Gospel and who is at the same time a member of the natural orders, the faith active in love penetrates the social order. Of the Christians Luther said: "The citizens of the kingdom of Christ are earthly, transitory, mortal men, live and dwell scattered here and there in the lands of this earth and are nevertheless at the same time citizens of heaven."[105] Only they truly understand the divine character of the natural orders.[106] And it is for the sake of the Christians that God maintains the world so

. . . .

monk and without fastings." (Tr. Loy)

[99] W.A., 32, 72, 26 (Sermons, 1530).

[100] W.A., 43, 30, 37 (Lectures on Genesis).

[101] W.A., 32, 142, 24 ff. (Sermon, 1530).

[102] W.A., 44, 326, 27 (Lectures on Genesis): "Verily, marriage is not such an easy life, but it is full of innumerable cares and burdens, full of sweat and hard work."

[103] W.A., 16, 359, 28 ff. (Sermons on Exodus, 1525).

[104] W.A., 37, 426, 34 (Sermons, 1534): "And this is true of all three realms (Church, State, Family), that each has its own devil."

[105] W.A., 45, 212, 21 (Sermons, 1537).

[106] W.A., 29, 599, 6 (Sermons, 1529): "This word, 'Give unto Caesar the things that are Caesar's, etc.,' godly Christians accept with gladness and gratitude because they are illuminated and instructed in regard to the character of government. . . . This

149

patiently. "He has indeed created all that the world contains and produces for the sake of pious Christians; He gives and maintains all only for their sake, as long as the world stands, in order that they should richly enjoy these things in this life and have no need."[107] Christians alone maintain both realms through their prayers.[108] Luther asserts: "We as Christians ought to know that the entire temporal rule and order stands and remains as long as it does only because of God's order and commandments and the prayers of the Christians. These are the two pillars which uphold the entire world. When these pillars are gone, everything must collapse, as will be seen on the day of judgment. And it is even now discernible that all kingdoms and governments are weakened and are beginning to topple because these two pillars are about to sink and break. For this is the way the

. . . .

peace (which government establishes) is such a great thing that nobody except the Christians gives it any thought and comprehends it."

[107] W.A., 22, 122, 30 (Kirchenpostille). Tr. Lenker. See also W.A., 29, 604, 16 (Sermons, 1529) and E.A., 5, 282: "That crops grow and there is peace on earth does not happen because of the godless multitude, but for the sake of the godly Christians. It does occur that the godless enjoy actually more peace than the Christians, for God is a rich and mild Lord who gives His goods to all the world, even to the godless, as Jesus says (Matthew 5:45), but it happens for the sake of the godly and grateful, even if the evil and ungrateful enjoy it also."

[108] W.A., 29, 604, 12 (Sermons, 1529) and E.A., 5, 282: "The Christians alone uphold the two kingdoms on earth, God's and the emperor's. And they do it with prayer. If there were no Christians and nobody would pray for these two kingdoms, they could not stand, even for one hour. In short, it is for the sake of the Christians that God spares the whole world."

[109] W.A., 45, 535, 3 (Sermons on John 14-15, 1538).

[110] W.A., 24, 273, 6 (Sermons on Genesis, 1527): "This is the answer to the question, 'How can a Christian bear the sword,

world wants it because it does not tolerate the Word of God (which honors and upholds the world) and persecutes and kills the innocent Christians and does not cease to rage against the very pillars which support it."[109] Yet God desires that the Christian take his full responsibility in the world. He may become a leader in secular affairs and even bear the sword.[110] If he attains political power he will at the same time govern his people and serve God.[111] Through the Christian in the world his faith active in love influences the social structure.[112] This Luther stated in the conclusion of his famous *Treatise on Christian Liberty*. He said: "The good things we have from God should flow from one to the other and be common to all, so that everyone should 'put on' his neighbor, and so conduct himself toward him as if he himself were in the other's place. From Christ they have

. . . .

since he is supposed to love everybody?' The Christian does not need the sword for his own sake and not for the sake of the other Christians either . . . but it is needed for the sake of the evil men. Since they must be stopped and the godly protected, a Christian, if he is called by God and by those who stand in God's stead, may go and kill like the others." W.A., 32, 390, 8 (Sermons on Matthew 5-7, 1530-32) "And this is another question, can a Christian take responsibility in this world and rule and administer the law? Is it possible that the two persons (Christian and *Weltperson*) or two kinds of office could be united in one man? Could one be simultaneously a Christian and a prince, judge, lord, servant, maid—which are simply persons of this world since they belong to secular rule? We say yes! God Himself has ordained and instituted secular government and its ranks. He has confirmed and praised it in His Word. Without it this life could not last, and we are all involved in it, indeed, born into it before we even became Christians."

[111] W.A., 51, 244, 34 (Exp. Psalm 101): "And God's help is especially present when David, i.e., godly, Christian princes rule. They serve God and rule the people at the same time."

[112] W.A., 47, 246, 37 ff. (Sermons on Matthew 18-24, 1537-40).

flowed and are flowing into us: He has so 'put on' us and acted for us as if He had been what we are. From us they flow on to those who have need of them. . . . We conclude, therefore, that a Christian man lives not in himself, but in Christ and his neighbor. Otherwise he is not a Christian. He lives in Christ through faith, in his neighbor through love; by faith he is caught up beyond himself into God, by love he sinks down beneath himself into his neighbor; yet he always remains in God and in His love."[113]

Luther could describe eloquently how under the influence of the Gospel a Christian ruler could make the institutions of secular authority the means of service. He suggested to the Christian ruler that he should imitate the example of Christ in his rule. Far from seeing in government merely a means of repression, he portrayed it as a glorious instrument of Christian service. Of the Christian prince, Luther said: "He must consider his subjects and rightly dispose his heart towards them in this matter. He does this if he applies his whole mind to making himself useful and serviceable to them, and does not think, 'Land and people are mine; I will do as I please,' but thus, 'I belong to land and people; I must do what is profitable and good for them. My concern must not be how I may rule and be haughty, but how they may be protected and defended by a good peace.' And he should picture Christ to himself, and say, 'Behold, Christ the chief ruler came and served me, sought not to have power, profit, and honor from me, but only considered my

. . . .

[113] Phila. Ed., II, 342 ff. (Treatise on Christian Liberty, 1520).

[114] Phila. Ed., III, 264 ff. (On Secular Authority).

[115] W.A., 10, II, 295, 27 (On Marriage, 1522). See also W.A., 10, II, 296: "In the same manner the wife should consider nursing, bathing, and all other care for her baby and all other work in which she helps and obeys her husband as truly golden and precious works. . . . And if a man should wash the diapers or do some other job which is commonly considered unfit for a

152

need, and did all He could that I might have power, profit, and honor from Him and through Him. I will do the same, not seek mine own advantage in my subjects, but their advantage, and thus serve them by my office, protect them, give them audience and support, that they, and not I, may have the benefit and profit by it.' Thus a prince should in his heart empty himself of his power and authority, and interest himself in the need of his subjects, dealing with it as though it were his own need."[114]

Similarly he described the faith active in love as it penetrates the difficulties and problems of married life. "What does the Christian faith have to say when confronted by marriage? It opens its eyes and sees all the humble and despised works that are part of married life and, looking at them spiritually, it becomes aware of the fact that they are all adorned with divine blessing as with gold and precious stones. And faith says, 'Dear Lord, because I know that Thou hast made me a man and a father, I know also that these works please Thee. And I confess that I am not worthy to put the baby to sleep or to wash its diapers, nor to care for it and its mother. How have I obtained such dignity that I may serve Thy creature and Thy holy will? I shall do it gladly, even if the works were far more humble.' "[115]

The Christian in the world lives for the purpose of helping others,[116] and through his very existence protects his fellow man from destruction. "If there were no Christians on this

. . . .

man, and everybody should ridicule him and consider him a sissy and henpecked, if he does these works with the conviction I pointed out above and in Christian faith—my dear friend, who has any reason to ridicule him? God and all angels and creatures smile, not because he washes diapers, but because he does it in faith. And those scoffers who see only the work, but cannot see the faith, ridicule God as the greatest fools on earth. Indeed, these scoffers scoff only at themselves and are the devil's sissies with all their cleverness."

earth," Luther says, "no city or country would enjoy peace; indeed, in one day everything would be destroyed by the devil. That grain still grows on the fields, that people get well after sickness, that they have food, peace, and protection they owe to the Christians. For we are beggars (II Cor. 6), yet are making many rich, we have nothing and yet have everything, etc. And it is true that whatever kings and princes, lords, burghers, and peasants have in this world they do not have because of their blonde hair but for Christ's and His Christians' sake."[117]

This explains Luther's personal attitude towards the social order. When he tried to reform schools and churches, restrain usury, counsel fair trade practices, and organize the rehabilitation of the poor, he merely put into practice what he had preached and tried to bring his Christian insights to bear upon the social order.[118] He did not believe that the Christian Gospel could become directly useful to society. The small number of true Christians made such a development unlikely. In order to transform society, Christ uses the Christian individual who lives a life of faith in this world of unbelief. In the believer the secular and the spiritual realm meet. Through him the ethical principle of Luther's social ethics penetrates the practical principle, and the insights of the Christian faith become relevant to society.

Roman Catholicism has confused the two realms of existence by claiming that the church, i.e., the ecclesiastical institution ruled by the pope, must dominate both realms. In this manner the empirical church organization claimed to be able to supply all practical norms for social ethics. The church of necessity became involved in all the all-too-human

. . . .

[116] W.A., 15, 703, 30 (Kirchenpostille): "On this earth man lives not for the sake of works, in order that they may be profitable to him, for he is not in need of them. . . . God does not desire the Christian to live for himself. Yea, cursed is the life that lives for self. For all that one lives after he is a Christian, he lives for others." (Tr. Lenker)

failings of its leadership. It had to give allegedly divine and eternal sanction to forms of social organization which were adequate for one age but which proved quite inadequate in another. Thus, for example, feudalism became the absolute norm for the organization of the state and patriarchy the absolute norm for the organization of the family.

The sects solved the practical problem of social ethics in two different ways. Some simply relinquished the world to the powers of evil and devoted themselves entirely to the contemplation of God and the enjoyment of their own salvation. Others attempted to enforce the Gospel as the law of the world. This made the Gospel a new law and perverted the essential message of Christianity. Since the interpretation of the Gospel as law varied greatly, even the New Testament used as the immediate source of social-ethical standards proved highly equivocal.

Luther, by emphasizing the theoretical separation of the two realms, avoided the identification of the Gospel with any specific program of social organization. By placing the individual Christian who alone is the proper object of the "good news" into the social order, he supplied the natural orders with a Christian social impetus that could exert constant pressure regardless of the particular form of social organization he might confront. Far from making Christianity irrelevant to the social order, Luther made it possible to make the absolute Christian truth ever available to society, not by means of an hierarchical organization or a legal interpretation of the Gospel, but by means of the Christian saint, i.e., the sinner saved by grace, active in the world as the willing tool of God's preserving and saving purpose.

· ·

[117] W.A., 45, 532, 11 (Sermons on John 14-15, 1538).

[118] The writings of Luther which show his social concern and his personal efforts in the direction of social reconstruction are so numerous that we can only refer to volume six of the Philadelphia Edition of Luther's works and to his many letters that deal with the problems of social reform and reorganization.

VII. THE LIMITING PRINCIPLE

No study of the principles underlying Luther's social ethics would be realistic if it dealt only with those ideas which according to Luther motivate social action. For an understanding of his thought it is of equal importance to examine that principle which more than anything else restrained Luther from advocating as thorough a reformation of the secular realm as he advocated and carried out in the spiritual realm.

Luther felt frequently that the social order needed reformation. He noted that the statesmen and lawyers were also in need of "a Luther" who would attempt to reform the existing organization of society.[1] He gave up all hope that under the law as practiced in his time justice could triumph. "In this life," he said sadly, "the lawyers catch the mosquitoes and flies, but the big hornets and wasps tear through their laws as through cobwebs."[2] And he complained bitterly that everybody cries for justice and law and the entire world is in an uproar for justice's sake; but the quest for justice merely causes war, murder, and strife, so that it could almost be said that the search for justice becomes the cause of all

· ·

[1] W.A., 51, 258, 6 (Exp. Psalm 101): "I am not impressed by the wiseacre (Meister Klügling) who knows all about secular law and who knows how to do everything better—though I must concede that it seems to me at times that government and its lawyers could well use a Luther."

[2] W.A.T., 1, 1 (2).

[3] W.A., 5, 100, 35 ff. (Comm. Psalms, 1519-21).

[4] Cf. Phila. Ed., I, 173, ff. (Treatise on Good Works); II, 57 ff. (An Open Letter to the Christian Nobility); III, 201 ff. (An Earnest Exhortation for all Christians Warning Them Against Insurrection and Rebellion); III, 223, ff. (On Secular Authority: To What Extent It Should Be Obeyed); III, 403 ff. (To the

injustice.[3]

Yet in spite of all these expressions of dissatisfaction with the existing social order, he showed a remarkable reluctance to take the lead in any thoroughgoing social reform, and often poured cold water on the enthusiastic political efforts of some of his associates. What was the reason for Luther's disinclination to become a social reformer? He was willing to give advice on any economic or political question when the occasion arose. He would lecture on price control, condemn unfair trading practices, advocate compulsory education and decent salaries for the teachers. He would exhort princes and peasants, soldiers and merchants—yet he refused to develop any comprehensive and all-inclusive plan for social reorganization.[4] Everything was merely his personal Christian witness, an attempt to bring his Christian insights to bear upon the problems of society.

The key to the understanding of Luther's reluctance to press for a complete reformation of society was his firm conviction that it was unbiblical to expect such a change so late in the history of mankind.[5] The social-ethical "quietive" which limits in Luther's thought the social-ethical "motive" of faith active in love, is his expectation of the speedily approaching end of this world. Though he was not fanatical on this point and would expressly state that such

. . . .

Knights of the Teutonic Order); IV, 9 ff. (On Trading and Usury and A Treatise on Usury); IV, 89 ff. (Preface to an Ordinance of a Common Chest); IV, 101 ff. (To the Councilmen of All Cities in Germany that They Establish and Maintain Christian Schools); IV, 133 ff. (A Sermon on Keeping Children in School); IV, 205 ff. (Admonition to Peace: A Reply to the Twelve Articles of the Peasants in Swabia); IV, 247 ff. (Against the Robbing and Murdering Hordes of Peasants); IV, 257 ff. (An Open Letter Concerning the Hard Book Against the Peasants); IV, 285 ff. (Exp. 82nd Psalm); V, 29 ff. (That Soldiers, Too, Can Be Saved); V, 75 ff. (On War Against the Turk).

[5] For an examination of some of the eschatological ideas in Luther's thought, see George F. Hall, "Luther's Eschatology,"

views were not to be considered articles of faith,[6] he personally believed that history could be divided into six parts. The first part covered the time from Adam to Noah; the second, Noah to Abraham; the third, Abraham to Moses; the fourth, Moses to David; the fifth, David to Christ; the sixth began with the coming of Christ and will last until the end of the world.[7] Luther was convinced that mankind had arrived at the very end of this last period. Against the astrologers, who defended a circular view of history and hoped that soon a new golden age would dawn, he asserted that the papal rule of the Roman empire was the final stage of the last period of history.[8]

It was this conviction that history had come to an end and that the second coming of Christ was near at hand which made Luther see in all attempts to reform society merely efforts to repair a social order doomed to collapse very soon. He said: "Since no other rule can be expected in (this final period of) the Roman empire as Daniel indicates (2:40), it is not advisable to change it. But let whoever is able to do so repair and patch it the best he can, while we still live, and punish abuses and put bandages and ointment on its pocks. But if you tear out these pocks unmercifully, nobody will feel the pain and the damage more speedily than the clever barbers who rather tear out the

. . . .

The Augustana Quarterly, XXIII, 1944, 13 ff.

[6] W.A., 42, 649, 7 (Lectures on Genesis): "These divisions are arbitrary, and must therefore not be accepted as articles of faith."

[7] Ibid., 649, 1 ff.

[8] W.A.T., 2, 636, 6 (2756a): "The end of the world is here. It has reached the dregs . . . the prophecies of Scriptures are all fulfilled, the Judgment Day cannot be far. . . . If one compares the time that is left with the time past, it is hardly the breadth of a hand, just a little apple left hanging on the tree. Daniel divided the history of the world into the empires of the Persians, Greeks, and Romans. The pope kept up the Roman empire. He was the

wound than heal it. Well, Germany seems to be ripe, and I fear deserves strong punishment. God be merciful upon us! If anybody can improve things I shall say my poor Pater Noster for him if only I could also add the amen. For I have said it again and again (but who will believe me until they have experienced it) that changing and improving are two different things. One is in man's hands and God's decree, the other in God's hands and the result of grace."[9]

Luther felt that this mending and repairing was important. But those who expect to move shortly from a dilapidated house into a stately new mansion cannot be expected to take their present discomfort too seriously. They will be satisfied to repair the leaking roof superficially and to stuff old clothes into the drafty windows rather than tear down the whole house and build a new one. Thus, he felt that Christians in this world are aware of the shortcomings of the present arrangement of society but they also know that a wonderful new home awaits them in the very near future. They cannot take the repair of their present domicile as seriously as those who consider it their permanent home.

Luther believed in social reform, and he tried to do what he could to help in the reorganization of society—but from his eschatological point of view he was unable to take amendments to the constitution of the social orders as he

· ·

final straw. Now he is collapsing. There are many signs in the sky, on earth there is much building, planting, and treasure gathering. The arts have reached new peaks. I hope the good Lord will put an end to everything and not regard the astronomers who claim that a new golden age will begin in the year [15] 40." See also: W.A.T., 2, 33, 5 (1297): "The Last Day is before our door. My calendar is used up." W.A.T., 2, 216, 11 (1791): "If we defeat the Turks, then Daniel's prophecy is fulfilled and the Last Day has arrived." W.A.T., 5, 110, 12 ff. (5375x); W.A.T., 5, 184, 4 ff. (5488); W.A.T., 5, 205, 19 ff. (5512); W.A.T., 5, 267, 8 ff. (5590); W.A.T., 5, 373, 6, (5826); W.A.T., 6, 135, 1 (6703a); W.A.T., 6, 253, 38 (6893).
[9] W.A., 51, 258, 12 (Exp. Psalm 101).

found it as seriously as some of his more secular-minded adherents. Whatever Luther taught and did was in his own mind an attempt to prepare men for the coming kingdom of God that would consummate history on the day of judgment.[10] It was at this point that Luther parted ways with the revolutionary minds of his age. The knights and peasants who were being crushed in the death throes of a disintegrating feudal society hoped that Luther would become the leader of a revolution which would restore their ancient privileges.[11] Luther was quite willing to help with word and deed in order to improve their lot. In his *Admonition to Peace* he said: "We have no one on earth to thank for this mischievous rebellion, except you princes and lords."[12] And a little later he continued: "If it is still possible to give you advice, my lords, give a little place to the will and wrath of God. A cart load of hay must give way to a drunken man; how much more ought you to leave your raging and your obstinate tyranny and deal reasonably with

. . . .

[10] W.A., 25, 88, 19 (Lectures on Isaiah, 1532-34): "Whatever we teach, order, and declare is done for one purpose only: that the godly should learn to expect the advent of their Saviour on the Judgment Day."

[11] Nothing could be more misleading than the claim that the reformation was the cause of the German peasant war. For an examination of this problem see Günther Franz, *Der Deutsche Bauernkrieg,* Munich, 1933, p. v: "The German peasant war does not stand by itself. It was preceded for two centuries by a long, uninterrupted series of local revolts. The peasant war can only be understood in the context of these 'predecessors,' as the last link in a chain of such revolutionary movements."

[12] Phila. Ed., IV, 220 (An Admonition to Peace, 1525).

[13] Ibid., p. 223.

[14] Ulrich von Hutten, Franz von Sickingen, and a considerable number of the lower nobility in Germany felt strongly that the Gospel (and their rights) had to be established by means of force if need be. As early as January 16, 1521, while Luther had every

the peasants, as though they were drunk or out of their mind. Do not begin a struggle with them, for you do not know what the end of it will be. Try kindness first, for you do not know what God wills to do, and do not strike a spark that will kindle all Germany and that no one can quench."[13]

When the historical situation, however, demanded a decision and he had to choose between social revolution and the reformation of the Church, Luther's choice was obvious.[14] He was unwilling to sacrifice the reformation of the Church and the preaching of the Gospel for the sake of a social and political revolution whose outcome at best could benefit men only temporarily. As the revolution proceeded without him, he was unable to understand how anybody could have the temerity to use the cloak of the Gospel to cover his revolutionary designs. And the wrath which Luther outpoured so profusely against the revolting peasants was the wrath of a man who felt that here were

. . . .

reason to expect a fate similar to that of John Huss, he wrote to Spalatin: "You see what Hutten wants. I would not fight for the Gospel with force and slaughter. The world is overcome by the Word, the Church is saved, and will hereafter as formerly be restrained without violence by the Word." (Smith, Jacobs, *Correspondence*, I, 442. See also Fritz Walser, *Die Politische Entwicklung Ulrichs von Hutten,* Berlin, 1928). Although Sickingen offered Luther protection and the possibility of a revolution which would have given all political power in Germany to Lutherans (see Luther to Link, July 20, 1520, Smith, Jacobs, op. cit., p. 341), Luther numbered him among the "Rottengeister." These "Rottengeister" he accused sharply of using the Word of God to gain personal advantage and the applause of the rabble. Luther's attitude towards the peasants is characterized by the same fear that the Gospel might be misused as a cloak hiding the quest for personal advantage. He said: "Peasants, burghers, and noblemen all use our teaching merely to scratch wealth together." (W.A., 40, II, 158, 22; Comm. Gal., 1535) Luther insisted that God is the enemy of both tyrants and anarchists,

161

people who gambled with mankind's chance to have the Gospel of Christ freely preached, in order to win temporary material advantage.[15]

Those who criticize Luther's position from the point of view of modern political liberalism or Marxism and attack him as politically reactionary because he chose to be a religious rather than a political leader, accuse him essentially of being Luther rather than Karl Marx. From a completely secular and sensate point of view, Luther's reliance upon the power of God seems nonsensical. But it was this "otherworldly" attitude, this complete reliance on God, which made the Reformation possible. Luther succeeded, while the revolutionary heroes, Muenzer and Sickingen, failed.

It has been shown previously that faith was the source of Luther's social ethics; it can now be added that it was also faith that made it impossible for Luther to take any social reform ultimately seriously. Faith was the "motive" and the "quietive" of his social ethics. It was the driving force behind all his attempts to reorganize society and at the same time the reason why all such attempts were in the background of his theological thinking.

It is unfortunate that most attempts to analyze Luther's thought have completely neglected to stress the importance of his eschatology for an understanding of his seeming

. . . .

and "arousing them against each other He brings about the destruction of both." (Phila. Ed., IV, 243)

[15] Phila. Ed., IV, 237: "Again it is not true when you declare that you teach and live according to the Gospel. There is not one of the articles (The Twelve Articles of the Peasants of Swabia) which teaches a single point of the Gospel, but everything is directed to one purpose: that your bodies and your properties may be free. In a word, they all deal with worldly and temporal matters." See also W.A., 28, 517, 28 (Sermons on Deuteronomy, 1529): "The peasants said in their revolt, we too want to wear fancy collars and golden chains, and eat partridges."

political and social conservatism.[16] It must also be granted that Luther's unrealized expectations of an immediate end of the world resulted in an unnecessarily superficial repair of the social structure of this world. It does make a difference whether one is going to inhabit a house for another month or another year. Though Luther was justified in not expecting any ultimate solution of the political and social problems that face mankind, a more thorough repair of the mechanisms that govern men would have made the position of the Church of the Reformation a great deal stronger during the great political and social upheavals that confronted her.

The emergency nature of the reorganization of society, which for Luther included the empirical church, made the princes "emergency-bishops" and proved a serious handicap to a sound development of the Lutheran Church. In 1542 Luther stated: "Our secular lords must now be emergency-bishops *(Not-Bischove)* and protect and assist us pastors and preachers (since the pope and his gang do nothing for us, but rather hinder us) so that we can preach and serve churches and schools. As Isaiah says, *'Reges nutricij tui,'* kings shall nourish you and queens shall nurse you. As it was done in times past almost too generously, and as it is still done where the Gospel has made the godly."[17] Luther never bothered to find a more permanent substitute for

. . . .

[16] See, however, Einar Billing, *Luthers lära om Staten,* Uppsala, 1900, p. 98; Gustaf Wingren, *Luthers lära om Kallelsen,* Lund, 1942, pp. 20 ff.

[17] W.A., 53, 255, 5 (Example, How to Consecrate a Christian Bishop, 1542). See also W.A., 53, 255, 26: "My most gracious lords, Duke John Frederic, elector, and Duke Ernst, have assented and promised as temporal rulers and patrons of the episcopal chapter of Naumburg that they will leave the chapter undivided and a separate corporation as heretofore and take nothing from it. They have done this, in fact had to do this, as patrons of the chapter in order to keep the churches of the

this emergency solution. The relatively small interest in world missions which plagued Lutheran orthodoxy for centuries to come was another unfortunate result of Luther's foreshortened eschatology.[18]

Luther himself realized the missionary responsibility of the Church.[19] He said: "A Christian does not only have the right and the power to teach the Word of God, but he has an obligation to do so, unless he is willing to forfeit his soul and bring upon himself God's wrath. . . . And when he

. . . .

chapter faithful to the holy Gospel and the known truth, as true emergency-bishops, in case such a chapter should deviate from the true path. And it is the considered opinion of their electoral and princely graces that this should become a true Christian example for other episcopal chapters, in case they desire to follow for their own sake and the salvation and benefit of their subjects." Cf. W.A.B., 8, 394 ff. (3312), March 19, 1539 (Luther to Gabriel Zwilling): "Now our temporal prince must be an emergency-bishop and emergency-official." See also W.A.B., 8, 396 (3313), March 25, 1539 (Luther to the Church-Visitors in Thuringia) and W.A.T., 4, 378, 25 ff. (4561). Since the Diet of Speyer, Lutheranism had drifted more and more towards a concept of church government which turned the administrative leadership over to the prince of the realm and his appointees. Regardless of the original intentions of the reformers, the practical result of Luther's belief that church government could be arranged with emergency measures, since the world would not last much longer, was the administrative domination of the church by the state. This had very unfortunate results in Germany, e.g., Prussian Union and "German Christians."

[18] In the Lutheran churches of Europe, foreign missions had to develop against the vehement opposition of "orthodoxy" and often outside the established church. For example, although Denmark possessed colonies in the East Indies as early as 1620, the leadership of the Danish Lutheran Church ignored the missionary responsibility which this implied for almost one hundred years. When Lutheran pietism pressed for missions, the leaders of the orthodox movement opposed every attempt to awaken missionary zeal within the Lutheran Church. The

is in a place where there are no Christians, he needs no other calling but that he is a Christian and inwardly called and anointed by God Himself. He is obligated to preach and teach the Gospel to the erring heathen or non-Christians out of his duty of brotherly love, even though no man has called him."[20] He also demanded missionaries, saying, "If all the heathen are to praise God they must know Him and believe in Him. . . . In order to believe in Him they must hear His Word. . . . In order that they might hear, preachers

. . . .

orthodox Lutheran faculty of the ill-fated university of Wittenberg spoke of missionaries as "false prophets," and Pastor Neumeister, a clergyman in Hamburg and author of the popular German hymn, "Jesus nimmt die Suender an," concluded an Ascension Day sermon, in which he had demonstrated to his own satisfaction that the so-called missions are not necessary in our time, with the words: "Vor Zeiten hiess es wohl: geht hin in alle Welt: Jetzt aber: bleib allda, wohin dich Gott bestellt." (In times past the message was, go forth into the world—but now, remain wherever God has called you.) Cf. Gustav Warneck, "Protestantische Missionen" in Herzog, *Real-Encyklopaedie für Protestantische Theologie und Kirche,* Leipzig, 1877-88. Luther's eschatology, which had prevented him from developing detailed ideas on the world-wide missionary task of the church, tended to confuse those followers whose slavish admiration for his words was equalled only by an enormous ignorance of his basic Christian concern.

[19] To the following cf. Walter Holsten, "Reformation und Mission," *Archiv für Reformationsgeschichte,* XLIV, 1953, 1. Luther's attitude towards missions has been the subject of considerable controversy. Some following Gustav Warneck (History of Protestant Missions, New York, 1901), claimed that basic theological considerations of the reformer prevented a missionary emphasis. Others, and especially Holsten, re-examine and question the entire motivation of the modern missionary movement from the theological point of view of evangelical Christianity.

[20] W.A., 11, 412, 11 (Power of a Christian Congregation, etc., 1523).

must be sent to them to proclaim God's Word."[21] And in relationship to the non-Christian religions which he knew, those of the Jews and the Mohammedans, he expressed considerable missionary concern. However, as in the case of the emergency-bishops, Luther seemed to think also of emergency-missionaries. The military prisoners of the Turks had in his opinion a very real responsibility for the conversion of their captors. From his eschatological point of view a thoroughgoing investigation of the missionary problems and methods was as unlikely as had been a basic solution to the church-state problem.

In order to understand Luther's eschatological position, one must remember certain basic tenets of his faith. He considered life an introduction to death and said that from baptism to the grave the life of a Christian is a process of dying.[22] Christians are merely "pilgrims" on this earth; their entire life is a pilgrimage, and they should live as foreigners and guests in a foreign land. It is dangerous to encourage in such visitors and strangers the false notion that the world is actually their fatherland. Luther said: "A pilgrim does not intend to settle in the country through which he passes on his pilgrimage and at the inn where he lodges overnight. His heart and thought are somewhere else. He takes his meals and buys his lodging at the inn, but he keeps moving towards the other place where he is truly

· ·

[21] W.A., 31, I, 228, 33 (Exp. Psalm 117, 1530).

[22] Phila. Ed., I, 58 (Treatise on Baptism, 1519): "So, then, the life of a Christian, from baptism to the grave, is nothing else than the beginning of a blessed death, for at the Last Day God will make him altogether new."

[23] W.A., 34, II, 113, 19 ff. (Sermons, 1531). See also W.A., 12, 321, 25 (Sermons on I Peter, 1523): "This is the opinion of the Apostle when he says, 'Dear brethren, I beseech you as sojourners and pilgrims.' Since you are one with Christ, as baked into one cake with Him, and His goods are yours and your misfortune His misfortune and He takes upon Himself everything that is yours,

166

at home. Thus Christians are foreigners and guests in this world, but citizens of another country and kingdom, where they have a permanent home."[23]

It was this sort of thinking, derived from his study of the Epistles of Peter, which made it impossible for Luther to attach primary importance to the cares of this world. If the Christian is a pilgrim in this world and if his true interest lies in his homeland, the coming kingdom of God, where he is a citizen, he cannot be ultimately concerned with the affairs of this world. He will participate in the essential activities of men that maintain life and order, even in the foreign land, but he will not become as excited about any of these functions as the person who considers this world his real home. The Christian, according to Luther, will not expect that the problems that ultimately concern him can be solved by means of a reorganization of the social order. This adds a definitely quietistic element to Luther's thinking. The social ethics of Luther has a detached air which prevents him from lightly overestimating the possible accomplishments of social reforms and tends to let him expect the solution of the real problems of the world through the intervention of God rather than the efforts of man.

But what were the reasons for Luther's keen eschatological expectations? It seemed to him that a close examination of contemporary history indicated that the rule of the

. . . .

for this reason you should follow Him. And you should live as if you were no longer citizens of this world. For your goods are not on this earth but in heaven, and if you should loose all temporal goods you still have Christ, who is more than all these things. The devil is a prince of this world and rules it, his citizens are the people of this world. Therefore, since you are not of this world you should act like a guest in a hotel, who does not have his goods there but just takes his meals and pays for them. For this is merely a thoroughfare, where we cannot stay, but we must go on. Therefore we should not use the goods of this world except to clothe and feed ourselves and then be gone to another land. We are citizens of heaven; on earth we are merely pilgrims

Anti-Christ had begun in this world and that the end was at hand.[24] Two factors contributed to this analysis of the situation. One was the power of the papacy, the other the power of the Turks.

The Renaissance popes ruling in Rome seemed to Luther a clear case of the Anti-Christ sitting in the temple of God.[25] The idea that the pope might be the Anti-Christ had dawned on Luther as early as 1519, when he wrote to Spalatin: "I am studying the decrees of the popes for my debate and (I speak in your ear) I know not whether the pope is Anti-Christ himself or his apostle, so terribly is Christ, that is the truth, corrupted and crucified by him in the decretals. I am terribly distressed that the people of Christ should be thus deceived by the semblance of laws and of the Christian name. Sometime I will make you a copy of my notes on the Canon Law, that you too may see what it is to make laws regardless of Scripture simply from ambition

. . . .

and guests."

[24] It is of some significance that Luther's eschatological utterances are not limited to his last years but can be found even in his earlier writings. W.A.T., 2, 31, 32 (1291): "Doctor Martinus was forty-eight years old in 1532 and he said, 'I have one more year to preach, but I am afraid I won't live that long. I hope I shall see the Last Day.'" W.A.T., 2, 216, 7 (1790): "In 1532 Melanchthon said to Luther that the emperor would live to the forty-eighth year. Luther said, 'The world won't last that long, the prophecies of Ezekiel stand against it.'"

[25] W.A., 26, 147, 27 (On Anabaptism, 1528): "Listen what St. Paul says to the Thessalonians: 'The Anti-Christ shall sit in the temple of God.' If the pope is the Anti-Christ, as I most certainly believe, he must not sit and rule in the place of the devil but in the temple of God. No, he will not sit where there are only devils and unbelievers, or where there is no Christ or Christianity, since if he is to be the *Anti*-Christ he must be found among the Christians." W.A., 50, 4, 26 (Preface to Barnes, *Life of the Popes*, 1536): "Slowly, after Christ had been abolished, His apostles and faithful witnesses followed and eventually there

168

and tyranny, not to mention the other works of the Curia, which are like those of Anti-Christ."[26]

What was merely a suspicion in 1519 became a firm conviction soon afterwards, and by 1521 Luther was ready to develop this idea at length.[27] Luther gave many reasons for this view. It seemed to him that the papacy miraculously fulfilled all the biblical prophecies referring to the Anti-Christ, and Luther never tired of pointing out the striking parallels. The pope prohibited marriage in many cases and also demanded abstention from certain foods with the claim that such actions would contribute to an individual's holiness. This seemed to Luther a clear fulfillment of the prophecies of St. Paul about the coming Anti-Christ.[28] Similarly, he pointed out that the Anti-Christ would claim and collect the wealth of the world for himself. This prophecy he saw also fulfilled in the pope.[29] Furthermore, the pope had substituted works and ceremonies for the

. . . .

came a new Christ, namely the Anti-Christ, sitting in the temple of God, with his new saints. He taught us to worship those which neither our fathers nor he himself nor we had known. And this precious new divinity he adorned with indulgences, churches, gold, silver, gems, and all kinds of precious objects. And he distributed the land freely to his worshippers as the Spirit had prophesied in Daniel."

[26] Smith, Jacobs, *Correspondence*, I, 170 (Luther to Spalatin, March 13, 1519).

[27] W.A., 7, 705 ff. (To the Book of Magister Ambrosius Catharinus, etc., with an Exposition of Daniel 8, on the Anti-Christ, 1521).

[28] Cf. Nicolaus Amsdorf's preface to the first volume of the Jena edition of Luther's works. St. Louis Edition, XIV, 480.

[29] W.A., 22, 192, 20 ff. (Crucigers Sommerpostille): "And especially the great rat king at Rome with his Judas purse, which is the great money gulch that in the name of Christ and the church has appropriated to itself all the possessions of the world. For he has reserved unto himself the power to forbid whatever

grace of God, had introduced masses, pilgrimages, and monkish rules,[30] and punished far more severely those who trespassed against his imaginary decrees than those who broke the word, law, and command of God.[31] The pope creates sin where Christ takes it away, calls those who do not worship him "heretics,"[32] and opposes everywhere clearly and consistently the will of Christ.[33] But the clearest sign of all was for Luther the papal claim to be the head of the church. Against this claim he asserted: "The pope is not the head of the church; otherwise the church would be a two-headed monster, since Christ alone is her head, as St. Paul says. The pope indeed is the head of the devil's false church."[34] Summing it up, Luther said: "The Roman Anti-

. . . .

he pleased and again to allow it for money, even to take and give kingdoms, whenever and as often as he pleased, and taxed lords and kings as it suited him. This is a much more infamous and barefaced perversion of the temple of God into a house of merchandise than was perpetrated by the Jews at Jerusalem. For it belonged to Anti-Christ, as is prophesied of him, to levy and collect for himself the treasures of the world; and St. Peter speaking of such a hoard in II Peter 2:3 says: 'And in covetousness shall they with feigned words make merchandise of you: whose sentence now from old lingereth not, and their destruction slumbereth not.' " (Tr. Lenker)

[30] W.A., 40, I, 300, 34 ff. (Comm. Gal., 1535).

[31] W.A.T., 3, 318, 17 (3443).

[32] W.A., 5, 195, 21 (Comm. Psalms, 1519-21): "If you do not want to be burned as a heretic you must worship this Satan and Anti-Christ, who appears under the pretext of the name of Christ, and praise his works as divine."

[33] W.A., 7, 763, 12 (Against Ambrosius Catharinus, 1521): "Since the pope creates sin where Christ abolishes sin, and establishes justice where Christ abolishes justice and chains consciences where Christ liberates consciences, in short, because he does everywhere the opposite, puts sin in the place of grace and the law in the place of faith, how can you still doubt that he is the legitimate Anti-Christ, the abomination standing where it

Christ is a servant of error, an apostle of Satan, the man of sin, and the child of perdition."[35]

This understanding of the position and function of the papacy became an important part of Luther's theology. It was not merely part of his polemic but apart from all personal animosity a sincere theological conviction.[36] Luther claimed that the persecution of the Gospel as carried out by the papacy was not merely the expression of papal ignorance, but the fulfillment of its proper function as Anti-Christ. The pope and his crowd were given to idolatry and servants of the devil,[37] and if the devil himself would rule in Rome he could not do any worse than the pope.[38] The papacy has introduced a perfect system to weaken

· ·

should not stand?"

[34] W.A.T., 2, 17, 18 (1266). See also W.A.T., 3, 119, 11 ff.; W.A.T., 3, 132, 26 ff. (2985); W.A.T., 3, 562, 18 ff. (3720).

[35] W.A., 5, 653, 10 ff. (Comm. Psalms, 1519-21).

[36] W.A., 12, 392, 14 (Sermons on I Peter, 1523): "You must be armed with Scripture so that you cannot only call the pope the Anti-Christ but also know how to prove it so clearly that you could die with this conviction and stand against the devil in death."

[37] W.A., 52, 177, 3 (Hauspostille, 1544): "The pope and his followers are therefore regular idolaters and servants of the devil. They not only despise the Word, but also persecute it, while they claim to be holy on account of their observances, their hoods and tonsures, their fastings and masses and similar arrangements."

[38] W.A., 54, 268, 31 (Against the Papacy in Rome, Founded by the Devil, 1545): "Indeed, if the devil himself should rule in Rome he could not do worse. If he ruled himself, we could bless ourselves against him (with the sign of the cross) and flee so that he could accomplish nothing. But since the pope has given himself over to him to serve as his mask adorned with God's Word, it is not possible to recognize the devil behind the mask. This is the wrath of God. Then all these things happened which his bitter, devilish, hellish malice against Christ and His church

171

Christ's kingdom and to promote the kingdom of the devil under the pretext of the name of Christ.[39] Claiming that he can bring all men into heaven, he has actually closed heaven to all men.[40]

Thus, asserting to be the vicar of Christ and closest to God, the pope became the vicar of the devil and farthest removed from God. "Was not this the fate of the pope when he and his followers imagined they were the vice-regents and representatives of and the nearest to God, and persuaded the world to believe it? In that very act they were the vice-regents of Satan and the farthest from God, so that no mortals under the sun ever raged and foamed against God and His Word like they have done. And yet they did not see the horrible deceiver, because they were secure and feared not this keen, sharp, high, and excellent judgment, 'The first shall be last.' "[41] Spreading such errors all over the world and collecting money for them, the pope proved clearly that he is the Anti-Christ.[42]

The powerful position of the papal Anti-Christ revealed

. . . .

could plan. Thus, he with his lies, blasphemy, and idolatry became our idol, which we worshiped under the name of St. Peter and Christ."

[39] W.A., 41, 140, 30 (Sermons, 1535): "But the pope has accomplished most and found the best method to weaken Christ's kingdom and to strengthen and increase the kingdom of the devil (though using the name of Christ and the Church). There is no doubt in my mind that the pope has turned infinitely more souls over to the devil than to Christ."

[40] W.A., 47, 457, 5 (Sermons on Matthew 18-24, 1537-40): "The pope has actually locked heaven for the whole world and at the same time he calls himself the servant of all servants of God, who desires to bring the entire world into heaven. This is good lying, he pretends he would like to see everybody saved and at the same time they are supposed to observe his nonsensical rules."

[41] W.A., 17, II, 140, 21 (Fastenpostille, 1525). (Tr. Lenker)

to Luther that this world was nearing its end. But this conviction was further strengthened by the appearance of the military might of the Turkish empire. The conflict of the Western world with the advancing Turks formed the colorful background of the Reformation. Threatening the empire from the East, the Turks were largely responsible for the inability of Charles V to stamp out the Lutheran Reformation. Since he needed the evangelical princes against this mighty foe, he was in no position to offend them by destroying their religious freedom. For this reason it would have been quite understandable if Luther had looked favorably upon these unwitting allies.[43] But nothing was further from his mind. To Luther the Turks were another indication of the impending end of the world. He saw also in the Turks the power of the Anti-Christ.[44] "The person of the Anti-Christ is at the same time the pope and the Turk. Every person consists of a body and soul. So the spirit of the Anti-Christ is the pope, his flesh is the Turk. The one has infested the Church spiritually, the other

. . . .

[42] W.A., 7, 375, 17 (Cause and Reason for All Articles, etc., 1521): "Let him who wants to do so doubt that the pope, who spreads more than enough of such errors in the world, and who takes land, money, and goods for them from all over, is the true and final Anti-Christ. I thank God that I know him."

[43] Luther was aware of the power-political implications for the Reformation of the threatening armies of the Turks. This is best illustrated by the following episode reported in the *Table-Talk*. A member of an imperial mission to the Turkish Sultan reported to Luther that Suleiman had shown much interest in Luther and his movement and that he had asked the ambassadors Luther's age. When they had told him that Luther was forty-eight years old, he had said, "I wish he were even younger, he would find in me a gracious protector." But hearing that report Luther made the sign of the cross and said, "May God protect me from such a gracious protector." W.A.T., 2, 508, 17, (2537).

[44] W.A., 42, 634, 16 (Lectures on Genesis, 1535-45): "And this interpretation agrees with what Daniel says about Antiochus and

bodily. However, both come from the same lord, even the devil."[45]

Historically, this fact seemed to be verified by their simultaneous origin. He said: "Pope and Turk started out at the same time under Emperor Phokas, about nine hundred years ago."[46] And he advised that the defense against pope and Turk should go hand in hand, since both are expressions of the power of the devil. He counselled Christians to pray against devil, pope, and Turk[47] and often compared the destruction wrought by the pope with the havoc worked by the Turks, explaining that in their efforts to destroy the Church of Christ they complemented each other. "The Turk," he said, "fills heaven with Christians by murdering their bodies, but the pope does what he can to fill hell with Christians through his blasphemous teachings."[48]

. . . .

Paul about the Anti-Christ. He will raise himself over everything that is God and over all worship. For the Anti-Christ, that is the pope and the Turk, does not raise himself above God as far as His divine substance is concerned, which is the unknown and hidden God as Isaiah calls Him. But they place themselves above God as He is preached through the Word and manifest through worship. For both (pope and Turk) do not only neglect the Word and worship of God but hate and persecute them."

[45] W.A.T., 3, 158, 31 (3055a).

[46] W.A.T., 3, 173, 121 ff. (3104b).

[47] W.A., 51, 608, 24 (Call to Prayer Against the Turk, 1541): "Heavenly Father, we have indeed deserved Thy punishment. But execute the punishment Thyself according to Thy grace and not Thy wrath. It is better to be in Thy punishing hands than in the hands of men or enemies. . . . But Thou knowest, Almighty God, Father, that we have not sinned against devil, pope, and Turk and they have no right against us or power over us to punish us. But Thou canst use them as Thy harsh rod against us, who have sinned against Thee and deserved all this misfortune."

[48] W.A., 30, II, 195, 15 ff. (War Sermon Against the Turk, 1529).

174

Their cooperation indicates the end of the world, for Scripture speaks of two cruel tyrants who will lay waste Christendom when the day of judgment is at hand.[49] And Luther asserted that "no kingdom has ever raged as murderously as the Turk; he is the last and worst expression of the wrath of the devil against Christ."[50] In his "Call to War Against the Turks" of 1529, Luther went into a detailed study of Scripture in order to establish the position of the Turks in regard to eschatology; as a result of his studies he believed that he could say with certainty that the Turk is the same as the Gog, mentioned in Ezekiel 38 and Revelation 20,[51] and a study of Daniel 7 convinced him that the Turks were the "little horn" that would pluck out three of the ten original horns or kingdoms mentioned by the prophet before the day of judgment dawns.[52]

. . . .

[49] W.A., 30, II, 162, 1 ff. (Call to War Against the Turks, 1529): "Scripture prophesies two cruel tyrants who will lay waste and destroy Christendom shortly before the Last Day. One will be spiritual, armed with deceit or false worship and doctrine, opposed to the true Christian faith and gospel. Daniel writes in the eleventh chapter that he will exalt himself above all gods and all worship, etc. St. Paul in his Second Epistle to the Thessalonians, the second chapter, calls him the Anti-Christ. This is the pope and his papacy which we have discussed in other writings. The other horrible tyrant is armed with the physical sword. Of him Daniel prophesies powerfully in the seventh chapter and Christ Himself in Matthew 24; when He speaks of a great tribulation such as has not been from the beginning of the world until now, this is the Turk. Since the end of the world is at hand, the devil must attack Christendom most terribly as a parting shot, before we go to heaven."

[50] Ibid., 162, 19 ff.

[51] Ibid., 171, 15: "There can be no doubt that the Turk is 'Gog' (Rev. 20:8 ff.) who has come from the country Gog or the land of the Tatars in Asia, as the history books prove."

[52] Ibid., 166, 30: "Daniel says that after the ten horns there will appear another horn, a little one among the ten horns. Here

The rule of the pope and the Turk and the general disintegration of society forebodes the end of the world;[53] this was Luther's firm conviction. Since he looked at world history from such an eschatological point of view, he could not expect the solution of the world-historical problems through the normal political activities of the human participants in this drama. On the contrary, only God's intervention could possibly bring about a real solution of the world's problems. This was clearly the time of the Anti-Christ and that meant that history was coming to an end.[54] The Christians, who realized that only God can save man from the power of the Anti-Christ,[55] would have to pray daily for the coming of this Judgment Day. Luther put it: "Oh, that only the day of our salvation and of the Last Judgment would come soon. I desire this day far more avidly than any physical liberation. For in this world we would always get another Mohammed and pope. It would be much better if everything would be overthrown and abolished at once, and with it all the misery and misfortune of this life, than any

. . . .

appears the Turk."

[53] W.A.T., 6, 306, 21 (6984): "When the Turk begins to fail a little the Last Day will surely come. For this is the way it must be according to Scripture. Then the dear Lord will come as Scripture says, 'When I shall come again I shall shake the heavens and the earth and then will come the desire of all Gentiles.' There is commotion enough in the political life at present. Lawyers never had more to do than just now." Cf. Ibid., 34 (6985): "I hope, since the Gospel is despised, that the Last Day is not far off, not more than one hundred years. . . ."

[54] W.A., 45, 46, 14 (Sermons, 1537): "The apostles call this last age the age of Anti-Christ for they saw through the Spirit that nothing of Christ would be left in the Church except His bare name. And also that the Anti-Christ would rule the Church."

[55] Ibid., 47, 19: "For as I have said in this last age, we cannot even hope that this Anti-Christ devil be overthrown and Chris-

mere temporal change."[56] This day alone would bring the final defeat of the powers of the devil. Therefore, "those who are true Christians have no reason to fear this Last Day but every reason to wish for it with all their heart. For as long as they live in this vale of sorrows they will have little peace and rest. Today they are plagued with one, tomorrow with another misfortune. Furthermore, the world is their bitter enemy and persecutes them cruelly. . . . This misery they cannot shed as long as this life lasts. But on the Last Day all this will cease and they will be delivered from all evil. For this reason, Scripture calls this day the day of salvation. And we have no reason to fear but rather should rejoice in the blessed and happy day of the advent and appearance of Jesus Christ our Lord."[57]

Luther claimed that in a sense the day of death is the day of judgment for each individual.[58] This he believed because "in the sight of God there is no counting of time, a thousand years are before Him as if it were one day. Therefore, the first man, Adam, is just as close to Him as the

. . . .

tianity be saved through the Roman emperor or some other great secular power, as it happened in Christendom in times past. On the contrary, the Anti-Christ must himself have the highest power on earth and in addition he must have all kingdoms of the world duty-bound to obey him."

[56] W.A., 44, 613, 20 (Lectures on Genesis, 1535-45).

[57] W.A., 17, I, 220, 35 (Sermons, 1525). See also W.A., 34, II, 474, 32 (Sermons of 1531): "Our daily Lord's Prayer teaches us that we should gladly desire the arrival of the Last Day. And we must cry unto God to revenge His name, blood, and goods on this desperate godless world. No Christian can or should pray differently. . . . Therefore, if you do not desire this day you will never be able to pray the Lord's Prayer or confess the Creed. For how can you say, 'I believe in the resurrection of the body and the life everlasting,' if you do not desire it? If you believe it you must truly wish it with all your heart and love the Last Day." Cf. W.A., 37, 617, 13 ff. (Sermons, 1534).

[58] E.A., 1, 126 (Hauspostille): "Every individual's death is, as

person to be born last, just before the Last Day." He said: "God does not look at time horizontally but vertically. . . . Our reason can see time only horizontally. We must start counting with Adam one year after the other until the Last Day. But before God all these events are in one heap. What is long for us is short for Him. . . . When a man dies, his body is buried and decays, lies in the earth and knows nothing. But when the first man is raised on the Last Day he will think that it hasn't been an hour."[59] At the same time, Luther was convinced that there would be a final day of judgment for the world which would also be a day of joy for the Christians since their suffering would then come to an end. "Therefore, although the signs shall appear fearful and terrible to you, when sun and moon disguise themselves, all creatures are mingled in confusion, and finally the world itself is full of fire, yet you shall not judge by such appearances, but know that this indicates something different, nay, the very opposite to you, from what it does to the ungodly world, which together with its prince, the devil, persecutes you, and does not fear the future judgment."[60] He continued: "As a Christian, you must have such thoughts about the signs of the Last Day, as if you were lying captive among enemies and murderers in a high tower, and your pious ruler should come and begin to besiege the tower with

. . . .

Augustine says, his Last Day."

[59] W.A., 14, 70, 27 (Sermons on II Peter, 1523-24).

[60] W.A., 52, 16, 15 ff. (Hauspostille, 1544). (Tr. Loy) Cf. W.A., 45, 44, 10 (Sermons, 1537): "We Christians all hope for this comforting and joyful advent of the glory of the great God, our Saviour Jesus Christ. (Now He is weak, poor, and despised and in His disciples ever more ridiculed, rejected, spit upon, beaten, crucified, and killed.) We hope that this day is before the gates and will make an end to the innumerable atrocities of the condemned papacy. . . . At this advent Christ will show and prove Himself as our life and hope as we even now believe and preach."

178

great power, so that everything should begin to fall around you; you would not be afraid of the noise and cannonading, but would much more rejoice, if you knew that it was for your redemption. Thus you should do here too, says Christ."[61]

The Christian must try to remain ever ready for this Last Day. His entire life must be lived in the direction of this day. "Therefore, examine your life, probe your heart to ascertain how it is disposed toward this day. Do not put your trust in your own good life, for that would soon be put to shame; but think of and strengthen your faith in order that the day may not be a terror to you as to the damned, but be your joy as the day of your salvation and of the kingdom of God in you."[62] To forget this day, or to refuse to pray for it would be nothing else but to reject the kingdom of God. To Luther, not to desire the day of judgment is the same as not to desire the kingdom of God.[63]

And here the seeming lack of success of the Gospel and the difficulties that confronted the Church at every turn became for Luther signs of encouragement and assurance that the end could not be far off. With great emotion he said to some of his friends, "God be praised, who has taught us to sigh for the day of judgment and to desire it. While still under the papacy, all the world feared that day, as their

. . . .

[61] W.A., 52, 20, 9 ff. (Hauspostille, 1544) . (Tr. Loy)

[62] W.A., 10, I, (2) , 114, 28. (Tr. Lenker) Cf. W.A., 14, 71, 31 (Sermons on II Peter, 1523-24): "You know that everything must pass away, both heaven and earth. Consider how you will have to be ready with a holy and godly life as you are approaching this day. Therefore, Peter describes this day as one that is coming even now so that they be ready, hope for it with joy, and hurry to meet it as the day that saves from sin, death, and hell."

[63] W.A., 10, I, (2), 113, 6 (Adventpostille, 1522): "From all this we learn how few there are who pray the Lord's Prayer acceptably, even though it is prayed unceasingly in all the world. There are few who would not rather that the Last Day would

hymns, like "Dies illa, dies irae, etc.," indicated. I hope that this day is not far off and we may still see it." Here he was interrupted by one of his listeners who mentioned that when this day approaches the Gospel shall nowhere be preached, since Christ had said that on that day He would not find faith on earth. Luther answered: "What does it mean that we have the Gospel in some corners? Keep in mind that Asia and Africa do not have the Gospel and even in Europe the Gospel is not preached among the Greeks or in Italy, Hungary, Spain, France, England, and Poland. That little speck, Saxony, will not prevent the coming of the day of judgment."[64] Thus the very predicament of man became for Luther a reason to hope that the day of salvation might be near at hand. Far from being discouraged he felt that it made the imminent coming of Christ more likely.

For an understanding of Luther's social ethics it is essential to remember always that he firmly believed that all history is merely life between the times.[65] Nothing that man can do can bring about the solution of the basic problems of humanity. It is foolishness to hope for salvation from the temporal and shortsighted efforts of man. He said: "The greatest foolishness is that we fail to consider God, His judgment, His wrath, and His eternal gifts, but only concern ourselves with temporal affairs."[66] To such foolishness he did not want to be a partner. This was the reason why his

. . . .

never come. This is nothing else than to desire that the kingdom of God may not come." (Tr. Lenker)

[64] W.A.T., 5, 22, 16 ff. (5237).

[65] W.A., 12, 293, 1 (Sermons on I Peter, 1523): "This age is the last time, as St. Peter says; it will last from the ascension of Christ to the Last Day. This is why the apostles and prophets and Christ Himself call it the last hour. This does not mean that the Last Day was to come immediately after the ascension but that after this proclamation of the Gospel of Christ no other Gospel could be expected. And nothing else will be revealed and declared than what has been revealed and declared. . . . Secondly,

contemporaries found Luther slow to warm up to any world-saving schemes initiated by men. He disavowed with equal fervor the political and social panaceas of peasants and noblemen, pope and emperor. To those, for example, who placed their hope for the future upon a victory of the emperor over the Turks, he said with biting irony: "Here you can see how a poor mortal, a future victim of the worms, like the emperor, who is not sure of his life for even one moment, glorifies himself as the true protector of the Christian faith. Scripture says that Christian faith is a rock, too solid to be overthrown by the might of the devil, by death and all the powers, that this faith is a divine power (Romans 1:16). Such a power should be protected by a child of death who can be put to death by any kind of disease? Help us God, the world is crazy. . . . Well, soon we shall have a prince who will protect Christ and then someone else will protect the Holy Ghost, and then of course the Holy Trinity and Christ and Faith will be in fine shape."[67] And about the efforts of the papacy to solve man's ultimate problems by political means, he said with equal scorn: "If I were a soldier and should see as the flag of my army the colors of a cleric or a cross, even if it were a crucifix, I would run away as if the very devil were after me."[68]

Though willing to do anything in his power to help the establishment of the best possible social order in a dying

. . . .

there is not much time left to the end of the world. As St. Peter says (II Peter 3): 'One day is with the Lord as a thousand years, and a thousand years are as one day.' Thus he tries to lead us away from our own way of counting time so that we may judge time according to God's schedule. In His eyes this is the last time and the end is upon us. What is left is nothing in the eyes of God."

[66] E.A., 6, 485 ff. (Hauspostille).

[67] W.A., 15, 278, 1 (Two Imperial Decrees, 1524).

[68] W.A., 30, II, 115, 1 (On War Against the Turks, 1528).

world, he was unable to hope that this society would ever be the kingdom of God. And he rejected every effort to identify any political cause with the interest of this kingdom. Essentially he believed that even the political difficulties of man can be solved only through divine intervention. "There is no other help against the Anti-Christ devil except that the Lord Christ finally address him with the authority of His divine power, 'Get thee behind me, Satan.' "[69] And it is God who eventually brings the tyrants with all their cunning plans to naught. Luther said: "We have heard of God's great miracles which He does for His own, namely those who trust in Him and believe His Word and promise. Even if at first He acts as if He might desert them altogether so that they would be swallowed up and perish, He nevertheless comforts them and helps them in all persecution. And finally He upsets the game of the tyrants, throws away their dice, tears up their playing cards, and brings them and all their plans to naught."[70]

This firm belief in God's impending solution of all human problems is the limiting principle of Luther's social ethics. It is brilliantly summarized in a sermon on the Epistle for the Third Sunday after Easter (I Peter 2:11-20), where Luther says:

"So should Christians in all stations of life—lords and ladies, servants and maids—conduct themselves as guests on earth. Let them, in that capacity, eat and drink, make use of clothing and shoes, houses and lands, as long as God wills, yet be prepared to take up their journey when these things pass, and to move on out of this life as the guest moves on out of the house or the city which is not his home. Let them conduct themselves as does the guest, with civility toward those with whom they come in contact, not infringing on the rights of any. For a

. . . .

[69] W.A., 45, 47, 29 (Sermons, 1537).

visitor may not unrestrainedly follow his own pleasure and inclinations in the house of a stranger. The saying is: 'If you would be a guest, you must behave civilly; otherwise you may promptly be shown the door or the dungeon.' Christians should be aware of their citizenship in a better country, that they may rightly adapt themselves to this world. Let them not occupy the present life as if intending to remain in it; nor as do the monks, who flee responsibility, avoiding civil office and trying to run out of the world. For Peter says rather that we are not to escape our fellows and live each for himself, but to remain in our several callings, united with other mortals as God has bound us and serving one another. At the same time, we are to regard this life as a journey through a country where we have no citizenship—where we are not at home; to think of ourselves as travelers or pilgrims occupying for a night the same inn, eating and drinking there and then leaving the place. . . .

"Let not the occupants of the humbler stations—servants and subjects—grumble, 'Why should I vex myself with unpleasant household tasks, with farm work, or heavy labor? This life is not my home anyway, and I may as well have it better. Therefore, I will abandon my stations and enjoy myself; the monks and priests have in their stations withdrawn themselves from the world and yet drunk deeply, satisfying fleshly lusts.' No, this is not the right way. If you are unwilling to put up with your lot, as the guest in a tavern and among strangers must do, you also may not eat and drink. Similarly, they who are favored with loftier positions in life may not, upon this authority, abandon themselves to the

. . . .

[70] W.A., 16, 18, 29 (Sermons on Exodus, 1524-27).

idea of living in the sheer idleness and lustful pleasure their more favored station permits, as if they were to be here always. Let them reason thus: 'This life, it is true, is transitory—a voyage, a pilgrimage, leading to our actual fatherland. But since it is God's will that everyone should serve his fellows here in his respective calling, in the office committed to him, we will do whatever is enjoined upon us. We will serve our subjects, our neighbors, our wives, and children so long as we can; we would not relax our service even if we knew we had to depart this very hour and leave all earthly things. For, God be praised, had we to die now we

. . . .

[71] W.A., 21, 342, 37 ff. (Sommerpostille). (Tr. Lenker)

would know where we belong, where our home is. While we are here, however, on the way, it is ours to fulfill the obligations of our earthly citizenship. Therefore, we will live with our fellows in obedience to the law of our abiding place, even unto the hour wherein we must cross the threshold, that we may depart in honor, leaving no occasion for complaint.' "[71]

Thus those who have their fatherland in the coming kingdom of God pray expectantly "Thy kingdom come," knowing full well that "the kingdom of God comes indeed of itself, without our prayer; but we pray in this petition that it may come unto us also."[72]

. . . .

[72] Jacobs, *Book of Concord*, I, 368 (*Luther's Small Catechism*).

VIII. CONCLUSION

Most discussions of Luther's social ethics are characterized by two divergent tendencies. They attempt to show either that Luther had no social ethics at all, since he placed society outside the influence of the Christian Gospel; or that his social ethics was purely pragmatic, accepting the social order of his day and thus helping to bring about the growth of capitalism and nationalism. In the preceding pages an effort has been made to free the study of Luther's thought from these artificially injected considerations and to understand his social thinking within its own context, with little regard to the part it may play in the dialectical system of some modern historian, theologian, philosopher, or economist. It has been attempted to approach Luther's social ethics not in terms of his particular views as expressed in specific historical situations but rather in terms of the principles that underlie his approach to society.

In the course of the investigation it has been shown that the claims that the Reformation or Luther created capitalism or nationalism cannot be substantiated, and that the emphasis upon the direct relationship of these great forces to the Reformation merely confuses the issue and makes the understanding of the origin of the Reformation, as well as capitalism and nationalism, more difficult. Luther's social ethics can be understood only within the framework of the principles that motivated his life and thought. It does justice neither to Luther nor to history to deal with the Reformation as if it were some metaphysical prime mover that can be used to explain the economic and political problems of our age. Luther's social thought must be understood as an integral part of his thinking and in the context of his entire approach to life.

If this road is followed, the following insights about Luther's social ethics can be gained:

186

I. Luther's approach to ethical problems is existential, not legal. The value of an action depends entirely upon the part it plays in helping or hindering the individual's relationship to God in Christ. All ethical standards are meaningful only in life. They are good if they serve to reveal God, and they are evil if they hide God from man. This is true of social ethics as well as individual ethics.

II. The motivating force behind all Christian ethics is God's love. Man receives God's love in faith and passes it on to the neighbor. Faith is active in love toward the neighbor. Faith brings us to Christ and makes Him our own with all that He has; then love gives us to our neighbor with all that we have.

III. God confronts all men in His Universe and demands from them obedience to the orders that He has ordained for nature. Thus not only Christians but all men are confronted by His social-ethical demands. Christian social ethics is not the esoteric teaching for the elite, but rather the God-given, i.e., best, practical way for all men to preserve the world from self-destruction until the day of Jesus Christ. Regardless of the world's attitude to the saving Gospel of Christ, it must for its own temporal preservation abide by God's natural law. Such obedience does not save man, but is conducive to the welfare of the commonwealth.

IV. The Gospel, as such, cannot be used to rule since it applies only to those who believe. It would cease to be the Gospel if it became a new law and were identified with any specific type of social organization. Yet through the person of the individual believer, who is related to Christ through the Gospel but is at the same time a member of the natural orders, faith active in love penetrates the social order. Through the Christian individual, be he peasant or prince, the inexhaustible resources of the Gospel become available to the social order.

187

V. All life, of individuals as well as of collectivities, is lived in the shadow of eternity. The social order is merely an interim order valid until the impending end of this world. All the ultimate problems of man's individual and social existence can be solved only when the coming kingdom of God ends all human history. Until that time, all human efforts are merely attempts to eliminate proximate evils. The ultimate evils that confront man can be overcome only through the parousia of Christ, the coming kingdom of God.

If Luther's social ethics is understood on the basis of the principles upon which it is founded, all specific answers to specific social problems of his time become relatively unimportant. They are primarily of historical rather than theological significance. However, the social ethical principles derived from Luther's existential understanding of God's revelation are of considerable interest for all those who desire to understand God's plan for the Christian in society.

Though not every specific answer that Luther gave to the problems of his age may be applicable in the modern situation, his approach will still be valid in principle. For example, confronted with the blandishments of the Turks, who wanted to use him and his movement against the papacy, and at the same time faced with the appeals of the empire, under the influence of the papacy, to use his power on behalf of a Christian crusade against the pagan Turks, Luther declined both invitations on the basis of his Christian conviction that the end never justifies the means. Here Luther's stand sheds some light upon the contemporary dilemma of evangelical Christianity called to choose between the totalitarianism of Moscow and Rome, for the sake of expediency.

Similarly, Luther's objection to all attempts to make the Gospel the law of the Christian state seems equally valid and urgent in our time.

Though he erred in expecting the end of the world in his time, acceptance of his emphasis upon the finiteness of all human efforts to solve even man's social predicament could have saved many an upright and noble man who in our time trusted in human solutions much anguish and despair.

Living his faith in love, Luther tried all during his life to bring his personal Christian witness to bear upon the decisions that confronted his society. From the ninety-five theses of Wittenberg to the quarrel of the counts of Mannsfeld at Eisleben, he never tired of living his social ethics, showing in his own life that through the Christian individual the Gospel penetrates the social order. It would have been well for Christendom if those who followed Luther's lead had been equally zealous to show their faith active in love.

IX. BIBLIOGRAPHY

Primary Sources

Book of Concord, The Symbolical Books of the Evangelical Lutheran Church, edited and translated by Henry E. Jacobs, 2 vols., Philadelphia, 1908.

Luther, Martin, *Ausgewählte Werke,* edited by Hans Heinrich Borcherdt, Munich, 1922-25.

Luther, Martin, *Briefwechsel,* Kritische Gesamtausgabe, vol. I ff., Weimar, 1930 ff.

Luther, Martin, *Correspondence and Other Contemporary Letters,* edited and translated by Preserved Smith and C. M. Jacobs, 2 vols., Philadelphia, 1913-18.

Luther, Martin, *House-Postil,* edited by M. Loy, 2 vols., Columbus, 1869-1871.

Luther, Martin, *Sämtliche Schriften,* herausgegeben von Dr. Johann Georg Walch, neue revidierte Stereotypausgabe, 23 vols., St. Louis, 1880-1910.

Luther, Martin, *Sämtliche Werke,* 67 vols., Erlangen, 1826-57.

Luther, Martin, *The Precious and Sacred Writings of Dr. Martin Luther,* edited by J. N. Lenker, 14 volumes, Minneapolis, 1905.

Luther, Martin, *The Table-Talk,* translated by William Hazlitt, London, 1902.

Luther, Martin, *Tischreden,* Kritische Gesamtausgabe, 6 vols., Weimar, 1912-21.

Luther, Martin, *Werke,* Kritische Gesamtausgabe, 56 vols., Weimar, 1883 ff.

Luther, Martin, *Works,* with introductions and notes, 6 vols., Philadelphia, 1915-32.

Secondary Sources

Allen, J. W., *History of Political Thought in the Sixteenth Century*, New York, 1928.
Althaus, Paul, *Staatsgedanke und Reich Gottes*, Langensalza, 1926.
Theologie der Ordnungen, Gütersloh, 1935.
Luther und die Politik, Gütersloh, 1940.
Luthers Haltung im Bauernkrieg, Basel, post-1945 (no date).
An Outline of Ethics, translated by A. B. Little, S. T. D. dissertation, Chicago Lutheran Theological Seminary, 1948.
Ante-Nicene Fathers, edited by A. Roberts and J. Donaldson, 10 vols., Grand Rapids, 1950-51.
The Apostolic Fathers, with an English translation by Kirsopp Lake, 2 vols., Cambridge, 1912.
The Student's Oxford Aristotle, translated by W. D. Ross, London, 1942.
Arnold, Franz Xavier, *Zur Frage des Naturrechts bei Martin Luther*, Munich, 1937.
Aulen, Gustaf, *Den kristna gudsbilden genom seklerna och i nutiden*, Stockholm, 1927.
Christus Victor, London, 1931.
Baillie, D. M., *God Was in Christ*, New York, 1948.
Bainton, Roland H., *Here I Stand*, New York, 1950.
The Reformation of the Sixteenth Century, Boston, 1952.
Barge, Hermann, *Andreas Bodenstein von Karlstadt*, 2 vols., Leipzig, 1905.
Luther und der Frühkapitalismus, Gütersloh, 1951.
Barth, Karl, *Die protestantische Theologie im 19. Jahrhundert*, Zürich, 1947.
Bennett, John C., *Christian Ethics and Social Policy*, New York, 1946.
Berggrav, Eivind, *Man and State*, Philadelphia, 1951.
Betcke, Werner, *Luthers Sozialethik*, Gütersloh, 1934.
Betzendörfer, Walter, *Glauben und Wissen bei den Grossen Denkern des Mittelalters*, Gotha, 1931.
Billing, Einar, *Luthers lära om staten*, Uppsala, 1900.
Our Calling, translated by Conrad Bergendoff, Rock Island, Illinois, 1947.

Binder, Julius, *Luthers Staatsauffassung,* Berlin, 1918.

Boehmer, Heinrich, *Luther and the Reformation in the Light of Modern Research,* translated by E. S. G. Potter, London, 1930.

Road to Reformation, translated by J. W. Doberstein and T. G. Tappert, Philadelphia, 1946.

Brandenburg, Erich, *Martin Luthers Anschauung von Staat und Gesellschaft,* Halle, 1901.

Brentano, Lujo, *Die Anfänge des modernen Kapitalismus,* Munich, 1916.

Der wirtschaftende Mensch in der Geschichte, Leipzig, 1923.

Bring, Ragnar, *Dualismen hos Luther,* Lund, 1929.

Förhallandet mellan tro och gärningar inom luthersk teologi, Lund, 1933.

Brunner, Emil, *The Divine Imperative,* translated by Olive Wyon, London, 1937.

Calvin, John, *Institutes of the Christian Religion,* translated by John Allen, 2 vols., Philadelphia, 1936.

Cambridge Medieval History, edited by H. M. Gwatkin and J. P. Whitney, 8 vols., New York, 1924-36.

Cambridge Modern History, 12 vols., New York, 1903-10.

Carlson, Edgar M., *The Reinterpretation of Luther,* Philadelphia, 1948.

Catlin, George, *The Story of the Political Philosophers,* New York, 1939.

Cave, Sidney, *The Doctrine of the Person of Christ,* London, 1925.

Clemen, Otto, *Flugschriften aus den ersten Jahren der Reformation,* Halle, 1906.

Creighton, M., *A History of the Papacy,* New York, 1901.

Denifle, H., *Luther in rationalistischer und christlicher Beleuchtung* Mainz, 1904.

Luther und Lutherthum, 2 vols., Mainz, 1904-09.

Deutelmoser, Arno, *Luther, Staat und Glaube,* Jena, 1937.

Diem, Harald, *Luthers Lehre von den zwei Reichen,* Munich, 1938.

Dittrich, Ottmar, *Luthers Ethik in ihren Grundzügen dargestellt,* Leipzig, 1930.

Dörries, Hermann, *Luther und Deutschland,* Tübingen, 1934.

Eger, Karl, *Die Anschauung Luthers vom Beruf,* Giessen, 1900.

Ehrenberg, Richard, *Das Zeitalter der Fugger*, 2 vols., Jena, 1895.

Elert, Werner, *Morphologie des Luthertums*, 2 vols., Munich, 1932.

Das christliche Ethos, Tübingen, 1949.

Ellwein, Eduard, *Vom neuen Leben*, Munich, 1932.

Erhardt, Eugene, *La notion du droit naturel chez Luther*, Paris, 1901.

Evans, Austin P., *An Episode in the Struggle for Religious Freedom*, New York, 1924.

Fanfani, Amintore, *Catholicism, Protestantism, and Capitalism*, London, 1934.

Forell, George W., *The Reality of the Church as the Communion of Saints*, Wenonah, New Jersey, 1943.

"Luther and the War Against the Turks," *Church History*, XIV, 4, 1945.

"Luther's View Concerning the Imperial Foreign Policy," *The Lutheran Quarterly*, IV, 2, 1952.

Franz, Günther, *Der deutsche Bauernkrieg*, Munich, 1933.

Genrich, P. W., *Die Christologie Luthers im Abendmahlsstreit*, Göttingen, 1929.

Gibbon, Edward, *The History of the Decline and Fall of the Roman Empire*, 6 vols., New York, 1900.

Gogarten, Friedrich, *Politische Ethik*, Jena, 1932.

Grimm, Harold J., "Luther and the Peasant Revolt," *Lutheran Church Quarterly*, XIX, 2, 1946.

Grisar, Hartman, *Luther*, 3 vols., Freiburg, 1911.

Gyllenkrok, Axel, *Rechtfertigung und Heiligung*, Uppsala, 1952.

Hall, George F., "Luther's Eschatology," *The Augustana Quarterly*, XXIII, 1944.

Harkness, Georgia, *John Calvin, the Man and his Ethics*, New York, 1931.

Harnack, Adolf, *Martin Luther in seiner Bedeutung für die Geschichte der Wissenschaft und der Bildung*, Giessen, 1883.

Harnack, Theodosius, *Luthers Theologie*, 2 vols., Munich, 1926.

Heim, Karl, *Das Gewissheitsproblem in der systematischen Theologie bis zu Schleiermacher*, Leipzig, 1911.

Heimann, Eduard, *Freedom and Order*, New York, 1947.

Hendry, George S., *God the Creator*, Nashville, 1938.

Herzog, J. J., *Real-Encyklopädie für protestantische Theologie und Kirche*, Leipzig, 1877-88.

Hirsch, Emmanuel, *Luthers Gottesanschauung,* Göttingen, 1918.

Holl, Karl, *Gesammelte Aufsätze zur Kirchengeschichte,* 3 vols., Tübingen, 1923.

Holstein, Günther, *Luther und die deutsche Staatsidee,* Tübingen, 1926.

Holsten, Walter, "Reformation und Mission," *Archiv für Reformationsgeschichte,* XLIV, 1, 1953.

Introduction to Contemporary Civilization in the West, prepared by the staff of Columbia College, 2 vols., New York, 1946.

Janssen, Johannes, *History of the German People at the Close of the Middle Ages,* London, 1896, 1925.

Joachimsen, Paul, *Sozialethik des Luthertums,* Munich, 1927.

Jordan, Herrmann, *Luthers Staatsauffassung,* Munich, 1917.

Jorgensen, Alfred Th., *Filantropi,* Copenhagen, 1939.

Kantonen, Taito A., *Resurgence of the Gospel,* Philadelphia, 1948.

Kautsky, Karl, *Communism in Central Europe in the Time of the Reformation,* London, 1897.

Kinder, Ernst, *Geistliches und weltliches Regiment Gottes nach Luther,* Weimar, 1940.

Köberle, Adolf, *The Quest for Holiness,* Minneapolis, 1938.

Köhler, Walther E., *Luthers Schrift 'An den christlichen Adel deutscher Nation,'* Halle, 1895.

Dokumente zum Ablassstreit, Tübingen, 1902.

Luther und Luthertum in ihrer weltgeschichtlichen Auswirkung, Leipzig, 1903.

Kolde, Theodor, *Der Staatsgedanke der Reformation und die römische Kirche,* Leipzig, 1903.

Köstlin, Julius, *Luthers Theologie,* 2 vols., Stuttgart, 1901.

Lamparter, Helmut, *Luthers Stellung zum Türkenkrieg,* Munich, 1940.

Lau, Franz, *Aüsserliche Ordnung und Weltlich Ding in Luthers Theologie,* Göttingen, 1933.

Luthers Lehre von den beiden Reichen, Berlin, 1953.

Lewin, R., *Luthers Stellung zu den Juden,* Berlin, 1911.

Lilje, Hanns, *Luther Now,* Philadelphia, 1952.

Lindsay, Thomas, *A History of the Reformation,* 2 vols., New York, 1926.

Link, Wilhelm, *Das Ringen Luthers um die Freiheit der Theologie von der Philosophie,* Munich, 1940.

Ljungren, Gustaf, *Zur Geschichte der christlichen Heilsgewissheit von Augustin bis zur Hochscholastik,* Uppsala, 1920.
Synd och skuld i Luthers teologi, Uppsala, 1928.

Lortz, Joseph, *Die Reformation in Deutschland,* 2 vols., Freiburg, 1949.

Luchaire, Achille, *Social France at the Time of Philip Augustus,* translated by Edward B. Krehbiel, New York, 1912.

Lunt, William E., *Papal Revenues in the Middle Ages,* New York, 1934.

Luthard, Ernst, *Die Ethik Luthers in ihren Grundzügen,* Leipzig, 1867.

Maritain, Jacques, *Three Reformers,* London, 1928.

Matthes, Kurt, *Das Corpus Christianum bei Luther,* Berlin, 1929.

McGovern, William M., *From Luther to Hitler,* Boston, 1941.

McNeill, John T., *Unitive Protestantism,* Nashville, 1930.
Christian Hope for World Society, Chicago, 1937.
"Natural Law in the Thought of Luther," *Church History,* X, 3, 1941.

Miller, Edward W. and Jared W. Scudder, *Wessel Gansfort, Life and Writings,* 2 vols., New York, 1917.

Mirbt, Carl, *Quellen zur Geschichte des Papsttums und des römischen Katholizismus,* 3rd ed., Tübingen, 1911.

Müller, Karl, *Kirche, Gemeinde und Obrigkeit nach Luther,* Tübingen, 1910.

Nathusius, Martin von, *Die Mitarbeit der Kirche an der Lösung der sozialen Frage,* Leipzig, 1904.

Nelson, Benjamin N., *The Idea of Usury,* Princeton, 1949.

Nicene and Post-Nicene Fathers, edited by Philip Schaff, 2 series, 28 vols., Buffalo, 1886 ff.

Niebuhr, H. Richard, *Christ and Culture,* New York, 1951.

Niebuhr, Reinhold, *The Nature and Destiny of Man,* 2 vols., New York, 1941-43.
The Children of Light and the Children of Darkness, New York, 1946.
Faith and History, New York, 1949.

Nygren, Anders, *Agape and Eros,* 2 parts, 3 vols., London, 1932-39.

Obendiek, Harmannus, *Der Teufel bei Martin Luther,* Berlin, 1931.

195

Olsson, Herbert, *Grundproblemet i Luthers socialetik,* Lund, 1934.

Pelikan, Jaroslav, *From Luther to Kierkegaard,* St. Louis, 1950.

Pfeffermann, H., *Die Zusammenarbeit der Renaisancepäpste mit den Türken,* Winterthur, 1946.

Pinomaa, Lennart, *Der existentielle Character der Theologie Luthers,* Helsinki, 1940.

Prenter, Regin, *Spiritus Creator,* translated by J. M. Jensen, Philadelphia, 1953.

Preuss, Hans, *Die Vorstellung vom Antichrist im späteren Mittelalter bei Luther und in der konfessionellen Polemik,* Leipzig, 1906.

Preus, Herman A., *The Communion of Saints,* Minneapolis, 1948.

Ranke, Leopold von, *History of the Popes,* London, 1852.
History of the Reformation in Germany, translated by Sarah Austin, London, 1905.

Robertson, Hector M., *Aspects of the Rise of Economic Individualism,* Cambridge, 1933.

Rommen, Heinrich A., *The Natural Law,* St. Louis, 1949.

Rupp, Gordon, *Martin Luther, Hitler's Cause or Cure,* London, 1945.
The Righteousness of God, New York, 1953.

Schapiro, Jacob S., *Social Reform and the Reformation,* New York, 1909.

Schilling, Otto, *Die Staats und Soziallehre des hl. Augustinus,* Freiburg, 1910.

Schöffel, J. S. and Adolf Köberle, *Luthertum und soziale Frage,* Leipzig, 1931.

Schneider, Ernst, *Martin Luther, sexualethische Anweisungen,* Kandern, 1926.

Schulte, Aloys, *Die Fugger in Rom, 1495-1523,* 2 vols., Leipzig, 1904.

Schwiebert, Ernest G., "The Reformation from a New Perspective," *Church History,* XVII, 1, 1948.
Luther and his Times, St. Louis, 1951.

Seeberg, Erich, *Luthers Theologie,* vol. I, Göttingen, 1929, vol. 2, Stuttgart, 1937.

Seeberg, Reinhold, *Aus Religion und Geschichte,* vol. I, Leipzig, 1906.

"Luthers Anschauung von dem Geschlechtsleben und der Ehe," *Luther Jahrbuch*, Wittenberg, 1925.

Sittler, Joseph, *The Doctrine of the Word*, Philadelphia, 1948.

Smith, Preserved, *The Age of the Reformation*, New York, 1920.

Sohm, Rudolf, *Kirchenrecht*, Leipzig, vol. I, 1892, vol. II, 1922.

Sormunen, Eino, *Die Eigenart der lutherischen Ethik*, Helsinki, 1934.

Spitz, Lewis W., "Luther's Ecclesiology and his Concept of the Prince as Notbischof," *Church History*, XXII, 2, 1953.

Stange, Carl, *Studien zur Theologie Luthers*, Gütersloh, 1928.

Steinlein, Herman, *Luther und der Bauernkrieg*, Munich, 1903.

Stephan, Horst, *Luther in den Wandlungen seiner Kirche*, Giessen, 1907.

Stomps, M. A. H., *Die Anthropologie Martin Luthers*, Frankfurt, 1935.

Stratenwerth, Günter, *Die Naturrechtslehre des Johannes Duns Scotus*, Göttingen, 1951.

Switalski, Bruno, *Neo-Platonism and the Ethics of St. Augustine*, New York, 1946.

Tawney, R. H., *Religion and the Rise of Capitalism*, New York, 1926.

Thielicke, Helmut, *Theologische Ethik*, vol. I, Tübingen, 1951.

Thomas Aquinas, *Summa Theologica*, translated by Fathers of the English Dominican province, 22 vols., London, 1920.

Toynbee, Arnold J., *A Study of History*, 6 vols., London, 1935.

Treitschke, Heinrich von, *Luther und die Deutsche Nation*, Berlin, 1883.

Troeltsch, Ernst, *The Social Teachings of the Christian Churches*, translated by Olive Wyon, 2 vols., London, 1931.

Törnvall, Gustaf, *Andligt och världsligt regemente hos Luther*, Stockholm, 1940.

Vogelsang, Erich, *Luthers Kampf gegen die Juden*, Tübingen, 1933.

Walser, Fritz, *Die politische Entwicklung Ulrichs von Hutten*, Berlin, 1928.

Waring, Luther Hess, *The Political Theories of Martin Luther*, New York, 1910.

Watson, Philip S., *Let God be God*, Philadelphia, 1948.

Weber, Max, *Gesammelte Aufsätze zur Religionssoziologie*, 3 vols., Tübingen, 1922.

The Protestant Ethic and the Spirit of Capitalism, New York, 1930.

Wiener, Peter F., *Martin Luther, Hitler's Spiritual Ancestor*, London, 1945.

Wingren, Gustaf, *Luthers lära om kallelsen*, Lund, 1942.

Winter, Ernst Karl, *Die Sozialmetaphysik der Scholastik*, Vienna, 1929.

Wolf, Ernst, Politia Christi, *Evangelische Theologie*, vol. VIII, 1948-49.

"Zur Frage des Naturrechts bei Thomas von Aquin und bei Luther," *Jahrbuch der Gesellschaft für die Geschichte des Protestantismus in Oesterreich*, LXVII, Vienna, 1951.

Wolff, Otto, *Haupttypen der neueren Lutherdeutung*, Stuttgart, 1938.

Wünsch, Georg, *Der Zusammenbruch des Luthertums als Sozialgestaltung*, Tübingen, 1921.

Evangelische Wirtschaftsethik, Tübingen, 1927.

Evangelische Ethik des Politischen, Tübingen, 1936.

ABOUT THE AUTHOR

George W. Forell was born in Breslau, Germany, the son, grandson, and great-grandson of Protestant clergymen. After studying philosophy and theology at the University of Vienna, he came to the United States in 1939 to continue his studies at the Lutheran Theological Seminary in Philadelphia. After his ordination as a pastor of the Lutheran church, he served parishes in New Jersey and in New York City, continuing at the same time his studies at Princeton Theological Seminary and, later, at Union Theological Seminary. From the latter he received the degree of Doctor of Theology.

Dr. Forell has been a member of the philosophy department at Gustavus Adolphus College, St. Peter, Minn., and professor of systematic theology at Chicago Lutheran Theological Seminary. He has been a guest professor at the theological faculty of the University of Hamburg, Germany, and the All-Africa Theological Seminary at Marangu, Tanganyika. At present he is professor of Protestant theology in the School of Religion of the State University of Iowa, Iowa City.

Other books by Dr. Forell are *The Reality of the Church as the Communion of Saints, Ethics of Decision,* and *The Protestant Faith.* He is the editor of Volume 32 of *The American Edition of Luther's Works* and a past president of the American Society for Reformation Research.